Daniel Fusco writes [...] future will be like for [...] an ever-changing cultural milieu. From his vantage point near San Francisco, he is living and leading ministry in what he describes as a "post-post modern" world. As his neighbor, I concur with his conclusions about our setting as a precursor to the direction of urban – and ultimately all – American ministry settings. The insights in this book will help you prepare for future ministry in cultural settings more and more removed from any Christian context. Read it to explain your current setting and as a road-map for future ministry.

—Dr. Jeff Iorg
President, Golden Gate Baptist Theological Seminary
Mill Valley, CA

As a native Californian, and as someone who has spent a good part of the last twenty years ministering in Europe, I agree with Daniel Fusco's assessment that much of the Western World is Post Post-modern. Exactly what that means, and how we as believers in Jesus Christ are to respond is what this book is all about. Anyone who is serious about reaching people for Christ knows that in order to do so we must first of all, know God, and secondly, we must know people and how they think. This book offers some good insight into the mind of Post Post-modern men.

—Brian Broderson
Calvary Chapel Costa Mesa, CA

Daniel Fusco is the real deal. He is an intellectual with both theological and philosophical underpinnings that enable him to address the future wisely while being courteous towards the past. Furthermore, he is a practitioner who lives genuinely among the people of one of America's most post- postmodern contexts. Daniel personally embodies the integrity and the integration he writes about, and for which this nascent world longs. This book is well worth the read.

—Linda Bergquist,
Church Starting Strategist and author of
Church Turned Inside Out: A Guide for
Designers, Refiners and Re-Aligners.
San Francisco, CA

While many are squabbling about the past, the future is being written. What I love about 'Ahead of the Curve' is that it gives the Church a glimpse of what's to come. Understanding the times we live in is a prerequisite for any effective leader and this book equips us do just that!

—Bob Franquiz
Lead Pastor, Calvary Fellowship
Miami, Florida
Founder, ChurchStrategies.com
Author of "Zero to Sixty" and "Watermark"

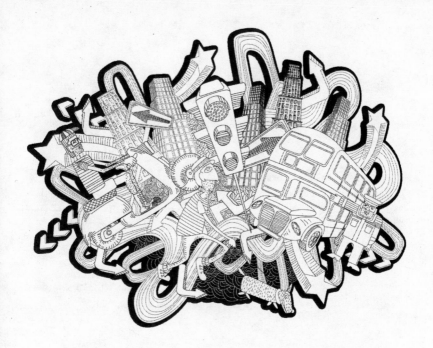

AHEAD OF THE
CURVE

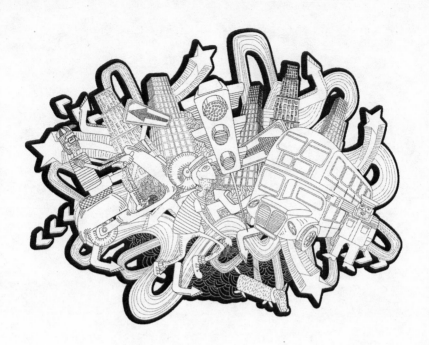

AHEAD OF THE
CURVE

Preparing the Church for
Post-Postmodernism

DANIEL FUSCO

TATE PUBLISHING & *Enterprises*

Published by Tate Publishing & Enterprises, LLC
127 E. Trade Center Terrace | Mustang, Oklahoma 73064 USA
1.888.361.9473 | www.tatepublishing.com

Tate Publishing is committed to excellence in the publishing industry. The company reflects the philosophy established by the founders, based on Psalm 68:11,
"The Lord gave the word and great was the company of those who published it."

Book design copyright © 2010 by Tate Publishing, LLC. All rights reserved.
Cover design by Lauran Levy
Interior design by Chelsea Womble

Published in the United States of America

ISBN: 978-1-61739-441-6
1. Religion, Christian Life, Social Issues
2. Social Science, General
10.12.15

Acknowledgments

Before we begin, it is important for me to acknowledge some of the many people I am indebted to. It goes without question that I am indebted to the Lord, for without Him, I can do nothing. It is hard to imagine what my life would be if He had not apprehended me along life's way and made me His child. Sheer grace is absolutely captivating and I am so grateful to be captivated.

In writing this book, I acknowledge that I am standing on the shoulders of many. Igor Stravinsky, the great Russian composer, is purported to have said, "Good composers borrow and great composers steal." I have gleaned so much from so many different people over the years but it is important that I acknowledge certain teachers who have been particularly foundational. Having grown as a Christian within the Calvary Chapel movement, I learned the Scriptures hearing expository Bible teaching. The amount that I have learned from Pastor Chuck Smith of Calvary Chapel Costa Mesa is immeasurable. His commitment to teaching the Scriptures simply gave birth to a movement and I am grateful to be a part of it. My pastor, John Henry Corcoran, now also of Calvary Chapel Costa Mesa, has been a great influence upon me. He trained me in and for the ministry and allowed me to grow. He taught me how to invest my life, and not just the gospel, in another person. In the last seven years, I have had the privilege of being able to study with many pastors through modern technological advances. There are also three contemporary Bible teachers who I want to acknowledge. Pastor John Piper of Bethlehem Baptist Church in Minneapolis, Minnesota; Pastor Tim Keller of Redeemer Presbyterian Church in New York City; and NT Wright, the Bishop of Durham, have all been formative in different ways in my theological understanding and ministry.

I want to thank the church bodies of Calvary Chapel New Brunswick, New Jersey, Calvary San Francisco, California, and Calvary North Bay, Mill Valley California, for their love and support. It is amazing that I get to love and serve alongside God's children and these three ministries are near and dear to my heart. Of special note is Professor Mark Wagner who I met when he was missionary in residence at Golden Gate Baptist Theological Seminary, Mill Valley. California. Mark greatly encouraged me to publish this work and I appreciate his friendship and insights. Steve Inskeep, our worship leader at Calvary North Bay, has also been very encouraging to have me publish this. Michael Graham, who serves Western seekers in India, has been a great source of both inspiration and challenge. He has encouraged me to not just preach theologically solid messages, but also messages that communicate within the budding worldview of the San Francisco Bay Area. I want to thank both Pastors Bill Walden and Tim Brown for taking me under their wings and keeping a close eye on me. I am grateful to be a *Timothy* to these seasoned men. I cannot thank Chuck Campbell enough for all that he is in my life. I am grateful both for his friendship and fellowship in the gospel.

A closing acknowledgment is to my beautiful bride, Lynn, and our beautiful children, Obadiah and Maranatha. I am humbled by your love and support. There is not a day that goes by that I do not thank the Lord for you.

Table of Contents

Introduction

Once upon a time, the Church of Jesus Christ established the direction that a culture would take. The ebbs and flows of ecclesiastical life would permeate secular life. People would look to the church to guide how life could and should be lived. Whether it be with respect to existential, moral, familial or other questions, people would look to their local churches to determine the answer. The church occupied a privileged position within society. But in the twenty-first century, this practice is a distant memory. The church is no longer any of these things. And far from defining culture, the church has fallen dramatically behind. No longer culture-shapers, the church is now at the disadvantage of trying to understand an alien, secular culture. Instead of shaping culture, the church is playing catch-up. The church does not understand our culture. It can scarcely be expected to shape it.

A steady stream of research and analysis being published reminds us of the tenuous position in which we find ourselves. *Newsweek* magazine, in its April 6, 2009 issue, ran an article entitled, "The End of Christian America." The article discussed the 2009 American Religious Identification Survey, which sought to understand the spiritual make up of America. This current survey found that the number of Americans who claimed no religious affiliation nearly doubled since 1990 to 15 percent. At the same time, the percentage of self-identified Christians had fallen to approximately 75 percent, a 10-percent reduction over the past twenty years.[1]

The article and the survey cited put hard numbers on the fact that Christendom is losing ground in America at a rapid pace. For commentary, *Newsweek* interviewed R. Albert Mohler Jr., the president of the Southern Baptist Theological Seminary. Dr. Mohler is a man I greatly respect and admire for his deep commitment to the things of God. In speaking of the survey, Dr. Mohler commented, "The most basic contours of American culture have been radically altered. The so-called Judeo-Christian consensus of the last millennium has given way to a postmodern, post-Christian, post-Western cultural crisis which threatens the very heart of our culture." Dr. Mohler is absolutely correct in noting that culture is changing. It is always changing. Cultures are never static because people are never static and culture is the collective understanding of masses of people. Cultures are as dynamic as the people who make them up. The problem, as I see it, is that Dr. Mohler stops short in his assessment. His comments read as if this postmodern shift is a recent development. It is not recent at all.

Modern evangelicalism is obsessed with postmodernism. There are books being written by the thousands on the subject. A recent search of an online website for major Christian bookstore revealed almost six hundred titles with the word postmodern in it. In ministerial circles, discussions on how to do postmodern gospel ministry are in full swing. Churches are reassessing and changing their approaches. Pastors are changing their delivery styles. There are global changes in ministry style, focus and approach, all trying to cope with postmodernity. But there is a problem. The problem is that postmodernism is not new. In fact, it has been around for decades. So why has it become the latest evangelical rage? It has ascended to a place of such prominence because in the last few decades postmodernism has permeated Middle America and the Bible belt where the greatest concentration of evangelicals is located. It is provocative to realize that both the East and West coasts were completely postmodern forty years ago. Forty years ago! Now that postmodernity has taken root in the center and the South, the discussions proliferate. But as was said earlier, cultures are dynamic, not static. So as great as it is that evangelicals are having the postmodernist discussion, the coasts have continued to evolve. The northeast and the west coasts are already post-postmodern, and that is the subject of this book. Christianity has fallen behind the curve and it is my hope that this book, in some way, will help to facilitate discussion to help evangelicalism get ahead of the curve.

You may be asking yourself, *How can you be so sure you are right? How do you know there are areas that are post-postmodern?* Let me share with you a provocative truth. In 2006, John Piper had a national conference in Minneapolis, Minnesota. The title of the conference was "Above All Earthly Powers: The Supremacy of Christ in a Postmodern World." The speakers included John Piper, Tim Keller, Mark Driscoll, DA Carson, David Wells, and Voddie Baucham, a veritable "who's who" of modern Christian thought. The conference sessions were powerful, informative, convicting, challenging and illuminating. *So what?* you may be asking. Let me explain to you the dilemma. In 1997, the University of Chicago had a conference called, "After Post Modern." This conference was also a seminal happening. But instead of the speaker list being made up of well known Christian ministers, the list was filled with philosophers, authors, and thinkers from various academic disciples all joined together to discuss where culture is heading after postmodernism. Nine years before a seminal Christian conference on postmodernity, the Academy was already having a conference on what is happening in culture as it moves past postmodernity. Nine years!

Do you see the problem here? The Desiring God conference put postmodern ministry discussions on the map of greater evangelicalism. Sure there were many conferences, writings and discussions going on well before the conference. But then it brought it to the center stage. As great of a conference as it was, I cannot help but think how much more helpful it would have been if it had been held twenty years earlier. It shows how behind the curve we had gotten. When evangelicalism has finally gotten the discussion to the masses, its successor was already ten years in discussion by academia. In many ways, it is like calling people for dinner when in reality, the host is already serving dessert and tea. Sure the main course is still available, but you are dealing with leftovers.

Papers published in connection with the University of Chicago After Post Modern conference confirm my presupposition. Gary Brent Madison, of McMaster University, writes, "If we absorb postmodernism, if we recognize the variety and ungroundedness of grounds, but do not stop in arbitrariness, relativism, or aporia [intellectual exhaustion], what comes after postmodernism?" Madison is getting at the heart of the Chicago conference. He is trying to understand where the dynamic culture has begun to head. The participants in the Chicago conference were seeing that culture was not going to stop evolving with mere relativism and arbitrariness. The intellectual exhaustion of pure relativism was untenable so something else had begun to happen. Do not forget these papers are now more than a decade old!

There are three essential elements that work together for successful communication. First, you have the content of the communication. For us, this is simply the gospel of Jesus Christ. Second, you have the deliverer of the message and how he or she decides to communicate it. This involves both language and style. Finally, you have the audience who will receive the message. In order to understand how to minister, we must first have a message that must be shared and decide how best to communicate that message in a way that the intended audience can understand.

For our discussion here, let us first address the content of the communication. As I have already mentioned, the gospel is unchanging so the scope of this book is not centered there. The gospel of Jesus Christ is unchangeable. It is fixed both in history and in the Bible. It should never be tampered with for it is the power of God on the salvation for all who believe. In our day and age, it is important to put that out there at the get-go. I fully subscribe to what is commonly understood as the orthodox and historic Christian faith. I hold these views without excuse. I hold fiercely to the inerrancy of Scripture, the deity of Jesus, the tri-unity of God, the virgin birth, and the visible return of Christ. All of these doctrines and many others are essential to the gospel.

It is within the second two components of communication that this book hopes to promote discussion. In many ways, the second two components of communication go together. They are in a symbiotic relationship. How we communicate the gospel is dependent upon who the audience is and vice versa. Each of the four gospels helps us to understand this. The spirit of God intentionally inspired four gospels. Each gospel tells the same story; that of Jesus Christ's sinless life, incredible ministry, his crucifixion, death, resurrection and ascension into heaven. This is the unchanging gospel. But a different minister was inspired to write each gospel. This accounts for the stylistic and content differences of the gospels. This was all according to plans and purposes of God. In John's gospel, there are shorter, terser sentences. Luke's gospel, because of his background in medicine, contains more technical language. Additionally, each minister was inspired to pen his respective gospel for a unique audience. This affects the presentation of the message as each audience had unique presuppositions and cultural understandings. Matthew's gospel was written for the Jewish people. There are an abundance of references to how Jesus fulfilled the Old Testament hopes of Israel for this very reason. John's gospel was written for the Greek mind where the discussion of the divine Logos is relevant.

The first half of this book will be focused on the third component, that is, on understanding the audience. It is my presupposition that in order for the church to get ahead of the curve of this dynamic culture, we need to realize that the culture in America is already post-postmodern. We need to understand our audience before we can communicate the unchangeable gospel to them in a meaningful and relevant way.

A simple analogy of this would be you shopping for a computer. When you go to the computer store, a good salesperson will immediately assess your level of understanding of computers if he hopes to sell you one. He needs to identify and understand your understanding of the topic so as to not be overly technical or overly simplistic in communicating the pros and cons of a specific computer. He needs to understand his audience in order to effectively communicate. The same is true for us. We need to understand this emerging worldview in order to effectively communicate the truth of the gospel to it. But if we get stuck trying to communicate to a postmodern audience when it is already past postmodernism, we will not be effective. So the first half of the book will be an attempt to explain this emerging worldview. The second half of the book will be focused on how we, as Christians who are committed to fulfilling the Great Commission, will communicate to this emerging worldview.

A final note, it is my hope that the greatest minds within Christendom will take up this mantle and search out a robust understanding of the emerging worldview. In no way do I expect this book to be the magnum opus on this subject. It is my desire to get the discussion started, a type of shot across the bow. I have not found any book that attempts to discuss that we are beyond postmodernity. Because of this, there is no attempt to understand what the main characteristics of this new worldview might be and how the body of Christ might respond with missional tact to the cultural changes that are upon us. I would not be writing this if people were already talking about it on a global scale. But this is my humble attempt to get the ball rolling. The message of love, hope and joy, this treasure that we hold in earthen vessels, is too important, infinitely more important than we can imagine, for us to take this subject lightly.

The Impetus for Discovery

Before we begin to discuss the emerging post postmodern culture and how we are to communicate with it, it will be helpful to understand who I am and what my experiences have been thus far. In chapter two, we will discuss the progression from modernity to postmodernity and beyond. There we will find that postmodernity's great critique of modernity was that it left the individual out of one's understanding of the world. So, in good postmodern fashion, it is important to understand who I am as an author so that you can understand the lens through which I am seeing the world.

I grew up thoroughly postmodern. I am part of the generation that was born in the mid 1970's and is currently referred to as either "Busters" or "Gen X." I grew up in a stereotypical northeast, middle class Roman Catholic family. Both of my parents were baby boomers and both worked full time jobs. My sisters and I were part of the first generation of latchkey kids. We lived in the suburbs, about forty-five minutes outside of New York City and were, for all intents and purposes, an average family. More specifically, we were the typical postmodern family. We were a Roman Catholic family in only the most nominal sense. We were taught that everyone was entitled to believe as they saw fit as long as no one got hurt. We were never taught the gospel of Jesus Christ or that He was the only way. My sisters and I played sports, acted in musicals, went on family vacations to the beach, and were normal American postmodern people.

By the time I reached high school, I was effectively an atheist, although not an intellectual atheist like the kind that is in vogue today. I was more of an apathetic atheist. I just could not care less about the potential of God. In many ways, I was purely secular but was ambivalent to the term. Although we occasionally went to church, it was just an hour to endure—nothing more. By sixteen years of age, I was a self-proclaimed hedonist. As a budding musician, my hedonism suited my self-aggrandizement well. In the fall of 1994, I enrolled at Rutgers University, in New Brunswick, New Jersey and continued in liberal arts studies. Rutgers is a well respected school and while I was a student there I was exposed to the best of postmodern thought. It was a fertile time for me intellectually, and an opportunity to explore and express my hedonism in more bold and reckless ways. Midway through my college experience, my mother was diagnosed with cancer. She subsequently died of the disease the summer before my senior year. My mother's death, which took place in the house of my upbringing, brought me face to face with an experience that I was wholly unprepared to comprehend. As a hedonistic atheist, I did not have the intellectual capacity to understand what I witnessed when I saw my mother take her last breath. I knew that her spirit had just left her body, but I could not have characterized it that way. As I stared at her lifeless body as it lay in the bed in our family room, I was struck by the fact that her body looked like her, but at the same time, was nothing like her. It was my mother's shell, but it was not my mother.

By this time, I had developed an appetite for philosophy, but that was of no help to me in this experience. I began to search and read the great books of religion and metaphysics from any tradition I could find. Whether it was the Bhagavad-Gita, the Tao Te Ching, the Koran or a plethora of New Age books, I was seeking answers to what I had experienced. I went to free vegetarian feasts with Hari Krishnas, tried yoga, and even tried visioning experiences while utilizing hallucinogens. I was searching diligently for answers to some of life's biggest questions. I kept swinging for the fences only to strike out miserably. During this season, I had two friends who began to follow Jesus. Their newfound faith prompted many discussions. They loved me dearly even though my lifestyle was wholly unacceptable to them. They were long-suffering through my many rants about the folly and curses of religion, still they always honored my questions with thoughtful and honest responses. They began to challenge me to read and study the teachings of Jesus. Little did I realize that they were actually teaching them to me over the course of our marathon spiritual discussions. I was also challenged to read the Bible by an adjunct psychology professor. I was trying to impress this professor with how well-read I was and he asked if I had read the Scriptures. I promptly replied that I had not. With great wisdom and tact he said, "Well you cannot be an intellectually honest skeptic unless you read Jesus' teachings." That, no doubt, was a challenge that I could not let pass. So in the early spring of my senior year, I began to read the Gospel of Matthew. Within a few months, I committed my life to Jesus Christ as the Lord imparted faith to me through His Holy Spirit.

It was already my plan to move to the west coast upon graduation. At the time, my focus was playing music professionally. In many ways, the easier road would have been to move into New York City to pursue a career in music. A close friend of mine and I decided to move to the west coast and devote some time to practicing and honing our respective crafts. We moved to Ashland, Oregon, and picked up part-time jobs to pay the bills so we could focus on music. This lifestyle was great for my newfound faith as I had ample time to read the Scriptures and pray. I was greatly encouraged by the few believers I knew to find a church, but I was not too passionate about the idea. Finally, I was invited to a church that I enjoyed and found the teaching of the Scriptures to nourish my soul. It was during this time that my faith and zeal in Christ was greatly stirred. The Lord was using many things to ignite a burning flame within my heart. As I was getting plugged into a fellowship, my music career was taking off. I was often on the road touring with my musical group. My pastor at the time encouraged me to take teaching tapes with me as I traveled and I would often listen to tapes over and over again. Playing music professionally gave me constant and continual access to the unbelieving and unchurched. My faith in Christ was often a topic of discussion and I would travel to shows with a bag full of giveaway resources, always hoping to be able to share the good news of the risen Christ.

As my faith grew, there were more and more confirmations that I was to enter the ministry of the Word. This came to a head in the fall of 1999 after I had moved to the San Francisco Bay area. I moved with the group with whom I was playing. When we first arrived gigs were scarce and I had ample time on my hands. So I devoted myself to fasting and prayer for direction and sensed that it was God's will that I devote myself entirely to the work of the ministry.

I was taken on staff at Calvary Chapel Marin, Novato,

California. Under the tutelage of Pastor John Henry Corcoran, I was given both extensive theological and ministerial training. Pastor John Henry was (and is) an anointed and passionate man. He relentlessly taught the Scriptures. In most areas, Pastor John Henry would see a church grow exponentially with his caliber of teaching and charisma. It is often said that sheep will always gravitate to the food. The only problem was that Marin County is one of the least churched counties in the United States. Less than 3 percent—that's right, 3 percent—of the population attends church on a Sunday morning. And that includes the church of Satan! Marin County sits quaintly between the city of San Francisco and the Sonoma and Napa Valleys and is also one of the wealthiest counties in the country.

After a few years I was sensing a call to church plant in New Brunswick, New Jersey where I had gone to college. I was gripped by the reality that I had not met another born again believer outside of my two friends. I never had anyone share the gospel with me. I had never heard of, nor been invited to, a church that was reaching out to a university that boasted of more than thirty thousand students. I felt that needed to change and in the summer of 2002, I was ordained and sent to plant a church there in New Brunswick.

Calvary Chapel New Brunswick was launched in September 2002. Here were the launch parameters: one person—me—and a budget of zero dollars. I found a job as a lunch shift waiter in a local restaurant and made just enough money to pay the bills. I stationed myself at a local coffee shop and spent every day building relationships and sharing the gospel. Although New Brunswick is a completely different demographic from where I had been in California, the situation was essentially the same. There were not many Christians there. Good Bible teaching could only get a church so far. All sorts of things needed to happen to get people to the church so they could hear good teaching. Folks, by and large, were not heading toward church or Christianity. They were, oftentimes, either hostile or ambivalent to the message of the love of God in Christ Jesus. The model that I had been taught, if you teach the Bible the people will come, was not working. There was something different going on. But what was it?

When you church plant with zero people and zero dollars, you really get an opportunity to watch the Lord work. It wasn't easy, but without a doubt it was amazing to see the hand of God at work. The church grew by ones and twos over the first few years. Watching the Lord provide a permanent worship location in the middle of the downtown area for almost nothing still causes me to bow my head and worship in retrospect. It was an urban church with a mixture of college students, yuppies, families and homeless people. There was a huge spread in age and socioeconomic status. My conversations day in and day out in the community were formative in my understanding of culture.

After three years, I was sensing that the Lord would have me turn over Calvary Chapel New Brunswick to my assistant pastor, Jason, and that I was to move on again. The ministry grew to almost one hundred people in four years. Some people may say that is nothing special. But it is important to note while I was there, and subsequently since I've been away, there have been two attempts by well known church planting outfits to try and plant churches in New Brunswick. Both used the most contemporary postmodern ministry approaches and both have struggled and chosen to move to a surrounding suburb. I don't say that by way of boasting, but instead to show that something post-postmodern was occurring. At the time I was in New Brunswick, I did not understand the phenomena. But that was about to change.

In November 2006, I moved to my present location, Mill Valley, California, to plant Calvary North Bay. Mill Valley is seven miles over the Golden Gate Bridge from San Francisco (and about twelve miles south of where I had been an Assistant Pastor). Really all of the research that will unfold in this book has been learned from ministering here. In planting Calvary North Bay, unlike my previous church planting experience, we had two families and a small budget for which I was very grateful. After about a year, Calvary North Bay had about fifty people. That may not sound like a lot to you, but for people who live in Southern Marin County, that number makes them very excited. You can count the number of evangelical churches in Mill Valley on one hand and at fifty people we had one of the largest.

I had been hearing for some time about a man named Michael Graham. Michael was recognized in New Age circles for being a long-standing follower of a well-known guru. He had had a radical conversion to Christ and was highly esteemed in the very small Mill Valley community of believers. He heard about Calvary North Bay and decided to come for a visit. After the service, he introduced himself and asked if we could get together sometime. That day we began a delightful friendship. One day over coffee, Michael shared some things with me that radically affected my ministerial life. In a nutshell, he told me that my teachings were great and that if I were ministering in the center or south of America, I would see the ministry explode. But I wasn't in the south, I was in Mill Valley. The area demanded a different way of communication in order to be effective. He told me not to be fooled by the fact that they speak English and drive BMWs. He shared that he felt that our ministry had a legitimate shot at making a dent in a community that was wholly unchristian, but he felt that it would not be possible unless I understood the audience I was trying to reach. With that exhortation, I grabbed hold of the challenge and have been running with it ever since. I continue to spend copious amounts of time trying to understand the worldview of the people who live in my community.

These ideas were crystallized for me when I was asked to share in two classes at Golden Gate Baptist Theological Seminary for my good friend, Dr. Mark Wagner. He wanted me to do a cultural exegesis on Mill Valley for his students as they were exploring spiritual warfare and its effects on evangelism. This opportunity gave me the opportunity to put all of my thoughts and research together in one place. Demographically speaking, I shared that Mill Valley was predominately Caucasian, extraordinarily wealthy, and extremely well-educated. But also has a suicide rate thirteen times the national average. With all of the affluence, education and privilege, something was very wrong.

As I moved from demographics to ethnographic identity, I shared that there were five defining characteristics of the average Marinite, with one overarching attribute that colors the rest. That overarching attribute is a general sense of entitlement. The simplest definition of entitlement is someone's belief that they are deserving of some particular reward or benefit. It is a sense that the average rules do not apply to them. This was brought into focus for me while working out at the local gym. It was a smaller gym and there are not many cardiovascular machines available. Because of their scarcity, those machines were hot commodities. There was a thirty-minute time limit on machines if there was a waiting list. There was one gentleman who, when he was on the waiting list, stalked the back line to make sure nobody goes over that limit, not even but a second. I watched in horror as he rudely chastised people for going over their time. Then one day there was a long waiting list and this man's time hit thirty minutes. I watched as he noticed his time and then looked at the waiting list. He then began to continually adjust his fan setting so that his time would not show on the display. When he was approached by someone on the waiting list about his excessive time on the machine, he was very angry and said, "Why are you asking me? What about other people?" When it was explained to him that since he was always so stringent with others about the time limit, he was singled out, he got off the machine very quickly and with much consternation.

This is a perfect example of entitlement. It was important to this man that he get on the machine, and that nobody go over the limit except him. The rules, at least in his mind, did not apply to him. He deserved some special treatment. This is the overarching attribute of my community. From that, the four characteristics are wealth, top-tier liberal education, buffet-styled spirituality, and excessively liberal morality and sexuality. I closed out the lecture by describing the implications of the demographics and ethnographic identity on the worldview of the average Mill Valley resident. It was here that I made the statement that Mill Valley is already post-postmodern. Our community is beyond pure pluralism and is into something radically new. Mill Valley was postmodern forty or fifty years ago.

After this lecture, Dr. Mark Wagner asked me again to come and take these findings to the next level and teach them in his Introduction to Missions class. He wanted me to move the discussion from the demographics and ethnographic identity of the city in which we live and focus more on this budding worldview. After sharing with his class, Dr. Wagner greatly encouraged me to publish this research and analysis in some form. So this is why and how I got here today.

As the coasts and the major metropolitan centers go, so the country will go. Dr. Tim Keller, in his message at the Desiring God Conference on the Supremacy of Christ in the Post Modern World, made a very lucid observation in explaining how the culture goes as the cities go. He said, in effect, that if the rural areas are Christian and the cities are secular, then you can expect the rural places to become more secular as the city folk migrate out from the country. He is right. As the cities go, so goes the culture. I believe the worldview that is prevalent in the Bay Area and northeast today will be the worldview of the rest of America in twenty-five or thirty years. This was true in the cultural shift from modernism to postmodernism and that trend will continue. It is important first that we understand what a worldview is and then what *this* worldview is so we can be ready and armed to share the gospel effectively.

Worldviews Create Worlds

How somebody views the world radically affects the world they experience. A worldview is a set of ideas or beliefs through which an individual, or culture, both interprets the world and interacts with it. This is why understanding how someone interprets the world affects how we communicate with them. Worldviews actually create the world in which someone lives. In using the word *create*, I do not mean it in the *ex-nihilo* sense in which God created the heavens and the earth in Genesis 1:1. In Genesis, God created everything out of nothing, thus the usage of the Hebrew word *bara*. *Bara* is used for God's initial creative act while *asa* is used of subsequent refashioning of the created material.

While we are discussing Genesis 1, it is important for us to see God's intention in creating mankind, and the created order out of nothing in order that we may understand how we, created in God's image, also create things. God created all the matter in the universe. The crowning jewel was the creation of mankind, whom God made in His image and likeness. In reading Genesis 2 and 3, we realize that being created in the image of God involves three main areas. God created man for relationship, stewardship, and worship. We know that we were created for relationship because of the relationship we see Adam having with God in the Garden, as well as seeing that the first thing in all of God's creation that was not good was that man was alone. Because of this latter issue, God declared He would make a helper comparable to Adam and created Eve.

We know God created man for stewardship by giving him dominion over God's created order in totality. Man was granted the responsibility to tend to God's created order as God's vice chancellor, much as Joseph was granted to tend to Pharaoh's kingdom. Finally, man was created to worship. God is glorious and man's soul is wired to exalt and uplift something. The fall of Adam and Eve was a worship problem. Worship, at its very least, means service with an ascribing of worth. When Adam and Eve disobeyed God, it showed that they worshipped something other than God. This is why the beginning of the Decalogue deals specifically with worship and idolatry. So God created man for relationship, stewardship and worship. When Adam and Eve fell, God's intention for relationship, stewardship and worship fell with them. The whole of human experience, from the beginning of humanity to the final judgment, is a playing out of this fall in time and space. Jesus was born of a virgin, lived a sinless life, suffered, died, rose again and ascended to the right hand of the Father to set right and restore humanity and creation back to that which God originally intended. Modern Christian thought acknowledges the restoration of worship to its original intention and emphasizes it. But much of this book will be exploring how the cross of Jesus Christ restores the areas of relationship and stewardship.

I have said that worldviews create the world, but in a different sense than that of God creating the world.

Indeed He created everything out of nothing. We, being created in His image with a creative spark, also create. But our creating is more like refashioning. We take existing materials and refashion them to make new things. Not absolutely new, but new in the sense that we, as humans, have not previously known, discovered, or fashioned them. A man and woman do not create the sperm and the egg, but they do create a new child as a product of their love and affection. A great composer does not create sound, ears that can hear sound, or rhythms; but he can reconstitute these already existing elements to produce beautiful music.

We call these people creative and they are. This is also true in how we see the world. For someone who is depressed, his melancholic view of the world around him, however it happens, creates a dreary and depressing world he not only sees, but experiences. We have often seen little children be inconsolable about not being able to find their favorite toy. Even when that toy is found, they are still inconsolable. This is because the way they are viewing the world actually is creative in a sense. Which is why it is important for us to understand the worldview of the people to which we attempt to minister. We must begin by understanding what the components of a worldview are, as well as how both modernity and postmodernity affect them.

The Center Leo Apostel for Interdisciplinary Studies' main topic of research is to understand how worldviews are constructed. The center's researchers at the University of Brussels have identified that a typical worldview comprises seven elements. The first element is ontology. Simply stated, ontology is a descriptive model of the world. This includes a description of the various elements that make up the world that is being lived in. Next, there must be an explanation of the world. Thirdly there must be a futurology. This concept simply answers the question, "Where are we heading?" Fourthly, a worldview contains values or answers to ethical questions. This concept within a worldview seeks to answer the question, "What should we do?" Next there is a praxeology, which is also commonly called methodology, or theory of action. It is a discussion and an understanding of how we are to attain the goals that are set before us. Sixth, any worldview has an epistemology, or a theory of knowledge. This is how we know what is true or false. Finally, a worldview must contain an etiology, which is an account of its own building blocks, origin, and construction.[2]

These seven elements may seem overly academic, but they make much more sense when we look at the Christian worldview in light of them. Ontology teaches us that the world contains, among other things, a Creating and Covenantal God, humans, the cosmos, and the angelic realm. The explanation of this world is that God created everything and sustains everything. Man has a place of dominion over the creative order. Man is affected by the angelic realm, but does not have control over it. Man has fallen and the creation has fallen with him. Our futurology teaches us that Jesus will return and there will be a final judgment. We look forward to heaven where there will be no tears or pain.

Our Christian ethic and values hinge on the greatest commandment: We are to love the Lord our God with all our heart, soul, strength, and mind. In like manner, we are to love our neighbors as ourselves. We have the great commission that encourages us to make disciples by going, baptizing, and teaching. Our praxeology teaches us that we are to attain their goals to the power of the Holy Spirit. We trust that all authority is being given to Jesus and that He will be with us even unto the end of the age.

Our epistemology teaches us that God's word is true

because God himself is true. The Bible teaches that God be true and every man a liar. We see obedience to the full revelation of sacred scripture as our only rule for life and faith. Our etiology shows us God as Creator and that we are fearfully and wonderfully made. God created the heavens and the earth and all the matter contained within it. It is important to remember that not everybody holds the Christian worldview, however. In fact, studies suggest that the vast majority of Americans do not hold this worldview at all. It is my attempt in this book to provide a framework for understanding this.

We need to put ourselves in the shoes of the non-believer. We need to think about how they see the world. We need to analyze how they interact with the world. Cross-cultural missionaries have been doing this for thousands of years. It is time, however, for us to apply the same skills here in the West to bridge the great divide within our culture. On any given Sunday, in most communities across America, there are vastly more people not going to church than there are in church. Fifty years ago, there was not as drastic a difference between the worldviews of the churchgoers and those of the non-churchgoers. But now there is a great divide, and in order to be effective, we must take the time to understand how the non-church-goers think and feel. We have just seen what makes up a worldview. Now we will take some time and look at what has made the twentieth century what it is, the worldviews of modernity and postmodernity. My intention in this book is not to be exhaustive in any sense of the meaning, but will briefly sketch some of the defining contours of both modernity and postmodernity so that we can see what this emerging worldview actually is.

Modernity is often called the Post Medieval period. It runs roughly from 1400 until about the 1930s. Historians tend to break modernity into an early and a later period.

The early modern period continues until about 1800. The modern era begins in the nineteenth century with the advent of industrialization. It is this latter period of modernity that has the most weight for us. It is what is commonly called the Enlightenment. The Enlightenment paradigm is also known as the "representation paradigm" in academic circles. Its goal is to see the world empirically. Reason has the upper hand. Proponents of modernity see the world as a mapping of what can be empirically understood.

Although the church seems currently obsessed with understanding postmodernism, I find it interesting to note that postmodernism began as an intellectual and cultural phenomenon in the 1920's. That was almost a century ago! Postmodernity's focus on social and political out workings has been the norm since the 1960's. The church is behind the time. We are trying to understand something that is nearly a century old, yet we still don't quite have a handle on it. Even the name by which we call the worldview, postmodernity, shows that we do not quite understand it. Think about the name of the first automobiles. They were called a *horseless carriage*. They didn't know what it was, but they knew it wasn't what they were used to. They had been used to horse drawn carriages and these new things did the same thing but without the horse. We call it *post-modernism* because we know that it is beyond modernism, but we do not quite know what it is still. This is more than a little disconcerting.

Tim Keller, the pastor of Redeemer Presbyterian Church in New York City, gave a basic outline of Western intellectual history in this way: Pre-modern (or Medieval) thought posits that we can know things truly through both reason and revelation. Modern thought believed that we can only know things truly through reason but not through revelation. But postmodern thought believes that we cannot know things truly either through reason or revelation.[3] This is what Gerry Grant Madison meant when he said Post Modernism leads to aporia or intellectual exhaustion.[4] This is why postmodernity is typified by relativism (there is not truth as it is all relative) and pluralism (one understanding is no better than another).

Postmodernity's great critique of modernism is that it left out the individual in understanding the world. The individual himself brings something to an understanding of the world. In many ways, this is why postmodern thought tends to be overly self-focused. Joe Queenan's book, *Balsamic Dreams: A Short but Self Important History of the Baby Boomer Generation*, is masterful at showing how self-improvement and self-centeredness is the predominant ideology of the boomers.[5] Postmodernity brought the self to the forefront of the discussion and obviously, the self enjoys the adulation. It has been commonly said that the postmodern worldview has three problems that must be overcome in order to do effective Christian evangelism.

You will notice that all three problems exist on individual and personal grounds. The problems are: the guilt problem, the truth problem and the meaning problem.[6] There is a guilt problem because most postmodern people do not have guilt over their mistakes because of their truth problem. They essentially do not believe in truth. Like Pilate, they ask the question, "What is truth?" It is a rhetorical question that assumes there is no such thing as truth. The guilt problem stems from the truth problem, which stems from their meaning problem. Because truth is relative and unknowable, how can anyone know what something really means? You can see how pure postmodernism leads to intellectual exhaustion!

Two of the main consequences of postmodern thought are the fragmentation of authority and the commoditization of knowledge. Postmoderns see things in terms of power plays. All authority is seen as an oppressive hierarchy. Karl Marx and Sigmund Freud's theories on this subject set the stage for what have now become readily accepted cultural beliefs. The whole situation is exacerbated by modern technology, which brings the world closer and makes it seem smaller. The Internet brings knowledge to us at a rapid pace. The postmodern person is used to having information from all over the world instantaneously accessible. This is a lethal combination. When distain for authority (and their truth claims) meet copious amounts of knowledge mixed with self-centeredness, the result is an inability to correctly assess meaning, truth or guilt.

Postmodernity, by and large, rejected on a grand scale, the empirical and rational claims of modernity. Postmodernists rejected truth and accumulated information. Postmoderns typify what the Bible speaks of when it says, "always learning but never coming to the knowledge of the truth." But as I look at the prevailing worldview of both the Northeast and the West Coast, I see something different than postmodernity. There is not the rejection of truth claims at all. But what is unique is that rather than rejecting what has come before, there is a prevailing sense that other viewpoints should be integrated into the worldview. Not just in an acknowledgment of viewpoints, but in the actual amalgamation of truths.

In the report from the After Post Modern Conference it says this:

> General statements of "truth" and objectivity' are permanently ambiguous—but this does not mean that truth and objectivity are lost. Rather they require more—they need a further contextual completion from what we are just then liv-

ing, before we can choose among variants for an activity at hand. Instead of mere pluralism, we can create "complexes of multiple truths" involving a demanding and sophisticated steering of scientific research with multiple applications and resonance to local contexts.[7]

It is these complexes of multiple truths that I see clearly on the coasts of our country. But this is just the tip of the iceberg. At this point, I am happy to introduce you to post-postmodernity. Let us give it a proper name. I would like you to meet the "Integral Worldview." What is it? Let us find out together.

The Integral Worldview: Putting a Name on Post-Postmodernity

At this point, you may be asking yourself, *Who coined the term, Integral?* Just as the tenets of modernity and post-modernity derive from the philosophers and pundits who advanced those views, so do the tenets and name of the integral worldview trace from their proponents. Originally, a man named Jean Gebser coined the term. He lived from 1905–1973 and at various points during his lifetime was a poet, linguist, cultural historian, mystic and philosopher. Currently the integral worldview is being actively discussed and promoted by psycho/spiritual/evolutionary teachers such as Ken Wilber and Andrew Cohen. Few Christians have ever heard of these men, yet Ken Wilber has authored over twenty books and is the founder of the Integral Institute, a think-tank for studying integral theory and practice. Andrew Cohen is the founder of *EnlightenNext* magazine (formerly called *What is Enlightenment?*). These men are well known and highly valued in many circles. Many psychologists and psychiatrists utilize their teachings and theories.

I will say from the outset, however, that narrative is not normative. Since we will be discussing these men frequently in this chapter, it is important that you realize that I am not promoting their teachings in any way. Nor do I think that their teachings will attain to any unique status within this emerging worldview. In some ways, they are teaching this worldview in its most pure and fundamental form. I do not believe that the pure form of their teaching will become the prevailing thought. It will be a more distilled and palatable version for the masses. But I do believe that many of the characteristics of their teachings have their finger on the pulse of this new worldview.

I will begin with Jean Gebser.[8] He believed that human consciousness was in the process of evolving. Gebser postulated five stages of development. The uniqueness of Gebser's theory was its evolutionary aspect. Each stage of development was a necessary antecedent to the following stage. There is not a rejection of the previous stage but an understanding that it was essential to make it to the next stage. The bulk of Gebser's framework was simply cultural exegesis. He looked back on human history, saw the predominant contours and wrote about it. But some of his ideas were also intuitively clear for what was coming after his context. We will now explore the stages themselves and their implications.

Gebser called his first stage the Archaic Stage. The stage is described as purely instinctual—instinctual in the sense that it describes humans in an animalistic state. Consciousness is seen as barely distinguishable from the environment in which we live in. Gebser notes that the Archaic Stage is seen most clearly in infants. From the Archaic Stage, human consciousness evolved to the Magic Stage. The Magic Stage is seen clearly in primitive tribal groups. This stage of consciousness utilizes the nature based religions and rituals and is often seen as the linking of the self with a small tribe or clan.

From the Magic Stage, human consciousness evolved to the Mythic (or traditional) Stage. In Gebser's model, this includes the great monotheistic religions of the world. This was the first time there was an awareness of soul. It also represents the expansion of the individual's identity to include an entire nation or belief system. From the Mythic Stage, Gebser believes human consciousness evolved to the Mental-Rational (or modern) Stage. This is the scientific rationality and reason of the Western Enlightenment. (I identified this stage in my discussion of modernity in the last chapter.) The focus of the Mental-Rational Stage is on the material world and objects outside oneself. But as we saw in the previous chapter, postmodernity was on the horizon.

Gebser's fifth and final stage was called the Integral Stage. A later Integral psychologist, Clare Graves, split Gebser's fifth stage into two distinct stages. Graves separated Gebser's final stage into the Pluralistic and the Integral stages respectively. This revised six-stage model is how things are presently discussed. The Pluralistic stage has its emphasis on multiculturalism and egalitarianism. Gebser calls it *aperspectivalism*. By this he means the pluralistic self's ability to see and appreciate multiple perspectives. Postmodernism is indeed aperspectivalism. But the final stage of consciousness according to this theory is the Integral, or post-postmodern, stage. This is the new worldview that has emerged in the Northeast and the West Coasts. Human consciousness is to be understood as evolving through a hierarchical series of distinct structures (each following the prior stages). In this Integral stage, evolution supersedes egalitarianism as the primary value.

Gebser studied the predominant trends of human history and charted culture shifts from almost no consciousness, to tribal/nature religions, to the great monotheistic religions, to the rationality of the Enlightenment, to the pluralism of Postmodernity and finally to a type of integrated perspective of them all. In many ways, Gebser surveyed the predominant trends in human history from a human consciousness perspective. He saw the origin of man and a shift towards a more tribal/nature/clan understanding. There followed a shift toward monotheism. Monotheism was (at least in some sense) replaced by rationalism, which was replaced by pluralism. Pure pluralism has been replaced already in many circles by the new Integral worldview

What Gebser refers to as the Integral Stage takes the rationality of the Enlightenment (modernity) and the culturedness/pluralism of postmodernity and adds to it an overarching spirituality. This allows people to integrate everything into a monolithic whole. Andrew Cohen describes this evolution of consciousness from egocentric to ethnocentric as a move from worldcentric to cosmocentric. What Cohen emphasizes in his characterization is that an individual becomes more connected, or aware, of his place within the whole of humanity and the world. Cohen theorizes that the early stages of the evolution of consciousness begins with a more individualistic framework. This gives way to a more micro communal mentality (whether it be a tribe, culture, or even a nation). The consciousness of human beings, however, is continuing to evolve, and pluralism gives us a worldcentric view. This aims at grasping the best parts of a pluralistic worldview, namely that there are other perspectives contained in a connected world. But it moves to a cosmocentric view, which is a person's connection not only to the whole of humanity, but also to the creation.

In this new worldview, the two main attributes that emerge are syncretism and spirituality. By spirituality, I mean an overarching bent toward discussions of metaphysics. By syncretism, I mean the incorporation and integration of other ideas that produce a different form of a belief structure. This is where Ken Wilber comes to the forefront of the discussion. His writings display that he has processed an amazing amount of information from many divergent spiritual, sociological, and psychological traditions. He is seeking to incorporate all that information into one cohesive whole. Postmodern thinking concludes that it is a person's prerogative to have spiritual beliefs if they choose to. But Integral thinking concludes that spirituality is essential to a healthy humanity and the earth, and that the incorporation of transperspectival and transdisciplinary thought is essential to being *fully human*. From this it is clear to understand why this line of thinking is called the Integral worldview. It is the integration of modern rationalism with postmodern pluralism with an emphasis on spirituality and syncretism. When you add this all together, you have a unique worldview.

I will list eight characteristics of the Integral worldview to add on to our understanding of post modernity, providing a framework for understanding post-postmodernity. First we will explore the spirituality and syncretism, and then examine six additional characteristics that flow from the first two.

The postmodern fragmentation of authority has given way to a new type of spirituality, one that I call *smorgasbord spirituality*. The *Newsweek* article I cited earlier states that the rising number of religiously unaffiliated Americans are more apt to call themselves spiritual rather than religious. In a *Newsweek* poll, 30 percent describe themselves this way, up from 24 percent in 2005. [9] The spiritual but not religious ideology is in full swing in American culture. Men like Eckardt Tolle and Deepak Chopra are writing best-selling books on the subject. Opera Winfrey's Spirit Channel podcast is one of the most popular downloads on iTunes. In this sense, Oprah is perhaps one of the world's most recognizable televangelists. The practice of yoga is widespread in many places. An increasing number of people consider themselves spiritual although will not align themselves with any traditional religious group.

People today are having many different *spiritual* experiences, although not biblically acceptable ones. Notwithstanding that prayer has been banned in public schools, many charter schools in the San Francisco Bay area where I minister, open their days with a few minutes of silent meditation and reflection. Spirituality is on the rise while Christianity is on the decline. I cannot stress enough that smorgasbord spirituality is the centerpiece of the Integral worldview. I call it smorgasbord spirituality because people pick and choose what they want to believe and practice. Much like a buffet where you can choose what foods to eat, Integral spirituality allows people to choose the spiritual beliefs and practices they want from a virtually unlimited set of options, and leave the rest. It becomes individualized in such a way that people can have what they want, in whatever configuration they want, without the authority of structure.

The second characteristic is syncretism, the incorporation and integration of other ideas that produce a different form of a belief structure. Here there is an emphasis on incorporation rather than rejection. In modernity, the emphasis was on rejection, that there are certain things that do not hold empirical water. In postmodernity, the emphasis is not on rejection as much as it is on ambivalence. There are many perspectives, but none can be grasped. In the Integral worldview, there is an overriding trans-perspectival approach—the desire to integrate and incorporate as many truths into one overarching system as possible. If you were to talk with people outside of the church, you will generally find they want to incorporate some of the truths of everything they have heard. We see this more and more as we witness the move toward a more holistic approach to human health. Everything is becoming pan-disciplinary. The world is moving away from a compartmentalized point of view to a more integrated and holistic one. Previously, you might have separate doctors for your physical and mental health, and a minister or guru for your spiritual well-being. Now, an increasing number of people are looking for a more holistic approach to human wellness. Doctors who draw wisdom from numerous disciplines are increasingly being sought out. Rather than having specialists in specific areas, people search for professionals who can treat them holistically—body, spirit, and mind.

The third characteristic of the integral worldview is the return of truth claims. This was something wholly lost in postmodernity. Do you remember the "complexes of multiple truths" quotation from the After Post Modern conference? The Integral worldview shows us the return of truth claims. In 2008, this was seen very clearly in the San Francisco Bay area with both the election of the country's next president and California's Proposition 8, which sought to amend California's Constitution to permit gay marriage. One would be hard-pressed to prove pure pluralism by the pervasive discussions about who should be the next president and how a person should vote on Proposition 8. In the prevailing point of view, there was only one way to vote in both contests. If you voted this way, you were right. If you did not, you were wrong and some people would say subhuman. Ironically, the San Francisco Bay area became the land of liberal bigots.

Because of the return of truth claims, the fourth characteristic of the Integral worldview is a type of evolutionary spiritual pride. If you read or listen to Ekhart Tolle or Ken Wilber, you will discover that they frequently talk about those on a lower scale of enlightenment. For those who do not hold the same smorgasbord spiritual truth claims, there is a growing animosity toward *non-inclusivity*. This animosity will only continue to grow. The difference between the animosity of postmodernity and the Integral view is that the Integral's animosity comes across more as pity.

The fifth characteristic of the Integral worldview is an emphasis on scientific foundations for spirituality. This is interesting as the religion versus science debate continues to rage in the church, in academia, and in the media. Increasingly, we are seeing the publication of studies and books discussing the scientific foundation for human spirituality. This exists on both sides of the argument. There are scientists who profess to be Christians, including Francis Collins of the Human Genome Project, who are writing books to show how science proves the existence of the Creator God. There are also atheistic scientists, like Sherwin Newland, whose books explore the scientific foundation for the human spirit, which is the will to do good in this world. No matter which side of the debate somebody stands on, both sides want to utilize the empirical research of science to prove their points.

The sixth characteristic of the Integral worldview is a move away from pluralism, the point of view that *all is good*, to pantheism, which says, "it all *is.*" The word *pantheism* comes from a combination of two Greek words. *Pan* means *all* and *theos* means *God*. Pantheism means, "all is God." Pantheism is a belief system that posits that God exists and interpenetrates every part of nature. Romans 1 speaks extensively of the human condition that would rather worship the creature rather than the Creator. Many people are recognizing the spark of divinity that can be seen in all that God created, but they are unwilling to acknowledge and worship Yahweh. Now we see the worship of sex, wisdom, nature, humanity, bodies and everything other created thing.

The seventh characteristic of the integral worldview is self-deification—excessive narcissism and self-centeredness. This is the natural extension of postmodernity's *reintroduction of self.* When you have an abnormal view of self, and a bent towards pantheism, you have self-idolatry. In self-deification we see the fulfillment of Satan's quest to make as many people as possible become like him. These people see themselves as the center of their own world and expect everything and everyone's attention to revolve around or center upon them. This is a principal reason why so many people are so unhappy today. When a person sets himself up as divine and nobody worships him, it can be very disheartening.

The eighth and final characteristic of the integral worldview is the reintroduction of the spiritual into the secular. I cannot say that it is the reintroduction of the sacred into the secular because what is being reintroduced is not sacred at all. As the pendulum continues to swing, we will see more and more people pushing for spirituality to be reintroduced into our everyday lives. I formerly worked at a company in the San Francisco Bay area that not only allowed spiritual practices on the job, but actively encouraged it. The CEO of the organization felt that by encouraging spirituality among the company's workers productivity would increase and overall *corporate health* would improve. The company sponsored group therapy sessions to promote wellness among employees. This may seem strange to you depending on where you live, but I believe that over the next 20 years, we will see more of this. Many public schools, as I described previously, now allow for a few moments of meditation or quiet reflection. The smorgasbord spirituality will permeate secular life.

I believe this is the worldview that is emerging on both the Northeast and West coasts. Over the last seven years, I have ministered on both coasts and this is what I see happening. Planting churches from scratch has given me a unique perspective on reaching culture because you are trying to see a group of people come together. When you are in an established ministry, you can often miss the cultural shifts, as you are busy about the work of the ministry. When there is already a congregation to tend to, you are often blinded to how different the world has become outside the church walls, because the members have a tendency to spend most of their time relating with people who are similar to them. It is my assumption that this Integral worldview will continue to spread throughout the entire country. Just as post modernity was entrenched in New York and San Francisco forty or fifty years ago and now is pervasive across the entire country, it makes sense that the Integral worldview will do the same thing in the coming decades. The Integral mindset is the integration of physical wellness, emotional and intellectual astuteness and experiential spirituality. The question for us as Christians is, "How will we respond?"

Getting Ahead of the Curve

The laws of physics and two thousand years of Christianity have taught us that the pendulum always swings back and forth. The church is in a continual state of reforming. There is always a reformation going on! In the book of Acts, the Lord poured His spirit out upon the Gentiles, through the ministry of Paul and much to Peter's dismay. The predominately Jewish apostolic church where Peter had his ministry did not quite know how to handle the inclusion of Gentile believers in God's plan of salvation. In Acts 15, we see the Jerusalem Council leading the reform of the church to fulfill God's call on believer's lives. The inclusion of Gentile believers in the church demanded an expression of Christianity that was different than what the disciples had grown accustomed.

As another example of reformation in the early church, persecution was the norm. The church sought to understand how to be wise as serpents and gentle as doves as the persecution became more intense. Some succumbed to the persecution and lapsed by rejecting Christ. Others were martyred for their faith. Once the persecution ended, the church was forced to deal with the brethren who had left the faith but wanted to be admitted again into the communion of the body of Christ. Again the church was reforming.

As Christianity later became the official religion of the Roman Empire, calling oneself a Christian was in vogue. The churches were full of people who were there because they were *supposed* to be there, or because it was socially advantageous. So what happened? The monastic movement began. People fled the institutional church looking for a less superficial expression of faith. Later, at the time of the Reformation in the sixteenth century, the return to the Scriptures radically affected how Christianity was practiced and its position in the world. As in previous periods, the church was continuing to reform. Each new era in the world demanded a reorientation of Christians. The advent of the Integral worldview is no different. It will demand a fresh expression of the bedrock truths of Christianity.

As the West enters the stage where the Integral worldview is the norm, the Church of Jesus Christ will have to reassess and reorient itself again, as it has for centuries. It is important to mention that what I'm going to recommend in summary in this chapter and then describe more fully in subsequent chapters, is nothing new. Really it is the integration (don't miss the irony there) of some of the best parts of modern and historic Christendom. The church must return to historic Christianity through the fresh expression of the essential truths of Christianity. I acknowledge that some people will always resist change. Some people will love change for the sake of change. My hope, however, is to begin the discussion of how Christianity needs to position and reorient itself so that not only will it be relevant in the coming decades, but that it can be for the world what Jesus intended the church to be. Jesus died on the cross so that we might be salt and light just as He is. This is my goal, as I believe it is His goal.

I have identified six areas where Christianity needs to reassess itself in order to be positioned for His glory with the emerging worldview. I am going to touch on the six areas in the chapters that follow. In each of the next six chapters, I will discuss each one individually, albeit briefly. It is my hope that the greatest minds in Christendom will take these areas and develop them more fully and completely.

The first of the six areas is the most important. Everything else flows out of it. The first and most essential characteristic of the Christianity that will impact the Integral worldview is a true experiential Christian spirituality. Jesus died on the cross so that people may know God. Knowing God is not only an intellectual experience. When you know somebody, you experience them.

The second characteristic of the Christianity that will impact the Integral worldview is a gospel-saturated emotional life. People often believe in Jesus but their emotional maturity is stunted. They are redeemed but emotionally stunted. When a believer has a true experience of God through Jesus Christ, that experience should radically affect how he feels and reacts to life's contexts. This plays itself out not only in good times and bad, not only in how we feel about ourselves, but also in how we feel about the world around us.

Third, to impact the Integral worldview, Christianity needs intelligence and humility in our spiritual discussions. There is little doubt that Christianity has intellectual credibility issues in the modern world. We are content with pithy phrases and do not take the time to think through many of the honest questions that seekers have. It is also essential that we develop a sensitive bedside manner while discussing hot-button issues with nonbelievers. I am frequently appalled by the lack of sensitivity and compassion that some Christians display when interfacing with the lost. Bedside manner does not mean not telling the truth. It means telling the truth in a kind, caring, and tactful way. When a surgeon needs to perform a surgery, he needs to make a cut. Both a scalpel and steak knife can make the necessary cut, but doctors use a scalpel because they know that the steak knife will cause added damage. Christians too often use little tact and pick up the steak knife instead of the scalpel. We need to use the brains that God has given us to discuss the things of God intelligently and with the humility that comes from realizing that we are all sinners saved by grace.

Fourth, Christians must learn how to possess our temples with honor. The body is the vehicle for our spirits to work in this world. Often we forget that our bodies are the temple of the Holy Spirit, but we leave the Temple in disrepair. Our spirituality must affect our body image. Is it Christ-like to love God and be poor stewards of our bodies? When we tell people how awesome God is and yet have no self-control, what does that living epistle say about the awesomeness of God?

Fifth, our experience with Christ should abound in our interpersonal relationships. We live in a difficult time for interpersonal relationships. Families are breaking down, relationships are falling apart, and people are more disconnected than ever. What is sad is that the church is mirroring the world in these matters. While Jesus died for a sinner, He redeemed him into a community. The cross of Jesus Christ puts people into a family and a family has relationship with itself. At the same time, the cross of Jesus Christ is the single greatest lesson in conflict management. As we experience the love of God through the Holy Spirit, our love for people should be conformed to His love. Because of this, those relationships showed look drastically different than the relationships of those who do not know Christ.

Finally, Christianity needs to reassess its stewardship of God's created order. The Green Movement is in full swing. A great tragedy is that Christians do not lead the charge. The Scriptures teach us that God's invisible attributes are clearly seen in the things He has created and that it all declares His glory. Unfortunately, too many value this slightly. When God created man, He created him for stewardship such that we would oversee God's creation. He did that because He knew that in every aspect of the cosmos there is a picture of Him. The church has often abrogated its responsibility to steward God's created order because its members long only for heaven. But this runs against Paul's simple saying from Philippians 1, "For me to live is Christ and to die is gain." Paul is talking here of the maximizing both of this life and the next life. We often want to emphasize one to the neglect of the other. We have become poor stewards of God's creation because we hope and long for our heavenly abode and abrogate our responsibilities. As long as He keeps us here, however, we need to be about the business of stewardship working towards God's will on earth as it is in heaven.

A True Experiential Christian Spirituality

When you ask even the most nominal Christian what it means to believe in Jesus, he will often say that it means your sins have been forgiven. This is true, but the forgiveness of sins does not occur in a vacuum. When your sins are forgiven, something astounding occurs. It has been rightly said that the gift of God's grace is the gift of God Himself. The purpose of the cross of Jesus Christ is to bring fallen humanity back into fellowship and relationship with God Himself. John Piper rightly states, "God is the Gospel." [10] So, although believing in Jesus means your sins are forgiven, it also means so much more. Being a Christian means knowing God experientially because through faith in Christ's finished work, a believer is adopted into the family of God.

The Bible is filled with accounts of people having a direct experience with God. Whether it is Adam in the garden, Abraham overlooking Sodom, Moses at the burning bush or Elijah hearing God's still small voice, the Bible recounts God's direct dealings with humanity. An important characteristic of Christianity should be God's people having a direct experience with the Almighty. You might think this is obvious. But we must ask ourselves, "Are we really experiencing God on a daily basis? Are the people who attend the churches that we pastor showing evidence of a vibrant and continuous relationship with God?" We all know the answers to these questions.

My emphasis on this point is not simply because it is the very reason that God sent Jesus to die in our stead. The experiential emphasis is also a major part of the Integral worldview. I will illustrate this with a simple example. I have a friend who lives in Marin County and operates a yoga studio. As I have sought to understand the people in my community, I have noted that the practice of yoga is not limited to individual personal wellness. Rather, the practice of yoga has become exceedingly commonplace and is pervasive in the local culture. Although religious in nature, it is often promoted in community centers and pharmacies. I had been peppering my friend with questions about yoga philosophy and motivation. Finally, she said to me, "Daniel, we can talk about yoga but really, you need to experience it for yourself. I can explain things to you but you won't really understand yoga until you try it."

She was not as interested in my understanding of philosophy of yoga as much as she wanted me to experience first-hand the benefits she found in it. I began to wonder why I had never heard of a follower of Jesus sharing the gospel of the risen Christ in the same manner. Why is it that I have never heard someone tell another person, "You need to experience Christ"? I believe it is because God's people, although understanding the finished work of the cross, are not tangibly experiencing the benefits of the cross themselves. In many ways, the Church of Jesus Christ is content with the mental grid and corresponding worldview of Christianity without its truest essence, the abiding presence of the Lord.

The gospel of Jesus Christ teaches that we were enemies of God because of our trespasses and sins but that the blood of Christ has brought us near. Jesus has reconciled us to the Father. Once reconciliation happens, a relationship begins. Jesus gave us His Holy Spirit to ensure our relationship with God that He bought by His death on the cross would abide. All the work has been done so that we might know God. God Himself ensured that we could know Him through the completed work of salvation, initiated, sustained and ultimately culminated within the Godhead. It is a tragedy that so few seem to really be having a strong relationship with the Lord.

I realize when someone begins to talk about true experiential Christian spirituality many people may get very nervous. This nervousness has its root in either insecurity or fear. We are insecure because we do not like to acknowledge that we are not really experiencing God. We can get away with speaking the truth (which is so important) without ever having to experience the truth ourselves. We rightly desire to walk our talk, but we hate to confess that we are not experiencing all that God is for us in Christ. We are fearful from having witnessed the excesses of experiential Christianity practiced in some tribes of Christendom.

It is never a good practice to base theology on a reaction to someone's errors. Reactionary theology is always non-biblical since its foundation in something other than the revealed truths of God in His word. We should instead seek *true* spirituality. By this I mean a biblical expression of the finished work of Jesus Christ. I am in complete and total agreement with the Westminster divines that says the Scriptures are the only rule for life and faith. Spirituality is not Christian spirituality if its foundation is not found in the Bible. But the description of the experience of the children of God in the Book of Acts is drastically different than twenty-first century Western Christianity. This must change both for the health of the body of Christ and for the global cause of evangelism. So let us look at the biblical expression of true experiential Christian spirituality.

The Psalms are among the most vivid expressions of experiential spirituality in all Scripture. The Psalms are often the go to place for Bible readers as they contain some of the most profound descriptions of the life of God in the souls of men. We read almost every human emotion displayed in the Psalms. The Psalms are a study in experiential Christian spirituality. Look at to Psalm 27:4, "One thing have I asked of the Lord, that will I seek after: that I may dwell in the house of the Lord all the days of my life, to gaze upon the beauty of the Lord and to inquire in His temple." It seems obvious that David's desire is not to live in a temple perpetually, rather it is David's desire to experience what Jesus spoke of in John 15 that he, David, may abide in Christ. The ability to gaze upon the beauty of the Lord is experiential. To inquire in His temple and to receive direction from the Lord is experiential. David's asking and seeking is not for proper theology intellectually, but for a soul theology. David longs to experience God and to see Him in all of His resplendent beauty.

One of my very favorite Scriptures is Psalm 73:25, which asks rhetorically, "Whom have I in heaven but You? And there is none that I desire upon earth besides You." Asaph, the inspired writer of Psalm 73, is struggling while watching the prosperity of the wicked. Asaph is in want and struggling while those who are in abject rebellion against God are in plenty at leisure. But then Asaph remembers the ultimate end of those who are gaining the whole world and losing their own souls, and he begins to praise God.

It is clear from such a statement that Asaph is not thinking that he would be content with simply a monotheistic
worldview. His desire is to know and experience God on
this side of eternity.

Luke's second writing in the New Testament is commonly called the Acts of the Apostles. Many commen-
tators make the point that it would be better titled the
Acts of the Holy Spirit through the Apostles. I am continually convicted and challenged reading how God moved
in and through the apostolic Church. Paul's Damascus
Road experience, as well as being caught up into the third
heaven, was no doubt a powerful encounter. Peter's experiences post-ascension were not mere mental images but
powerful experiences of God. The day of Pentecost stands
out firmly in experiential theology. There are numerous
examples recorded in sacred Scripture of how experiential
the early Christian faith was.

The apostle Paul in the book of Romans says, "As
many as are led by the Spirit of God, these are the sons
of God." Being led by the Third Person of the Trinity is
the main characteristic of being a member of the family of
God. These types of experiences need to be sought after,
asked for continually, and we will find, receive, and be
opened for. The twenty-first century church has an utter
need for the true charismata. And the power encounters
need to begin in the church before we can ever hope for
them to begin outside of the church.

As I talk to people in my community about the gospel
and about evangelicals, I often hear how Christianity is
full of mental images without a corresponding confirm-
ing experience. Acts teaches us that signs and wonders
authenticated the message of the gospel. Most of us want
to wiggle around this fact because we have never seen or
experienced signs and wonders. We want to excuse them
because we know that no heart was ever changed sim-

ply by witnessing a miraculous event. But would it not be amazing if God's people were experiencing God in such a profound way as to have the potential for these types of events to follow? Not some sort of spectacle that appeals to the basest parts of human nature as is often the case, but instead a true and dynamic display of the power of God in the life of the person. The emerging Integral worldview sees experience as more powerful than just thoughts. Culture has become more and more experientially driven. We should not simply dismiss this as Christians. Because of the finished work of Jesus, Christians have the greatest potential for true spiritual experience.

As we seek to lay out the five additional areas where Christianity must reassess itself, as we continue to engage a dynamic culture, it is important to note that this first characteristic of true experiential Christian spirituality is the only absolute necessity. Everything else that follows will be the integration of this experiential truth into various areas of human experience. When someone has been profoundly affected by a biblical experience of God through the finished work of the cross and the ministry of the Holy Spirit, the experience will affect other areas of his life.

A Gospel-Saturated Emotional Life

We have all met people in church who believe and love Jesus but are emotionally immature. They understand the gospel, they understand the finished work, they believe in the Scriptures and they believe that Jesus will return. Despite all this, they are emotionally underdeveloped. This is not a judgment on them, it is rather assessment based upon experience. Their emotional lives have not been changed by their knowledge of God or the gospel. We are all in the process of being sanctified, being set apart for the Master's use. This is the work of God, which He does in us and to us for His good pleasure. Sanctification happens in His timing and not ours.

But there are also individuals whose emotional lives are out of step with the Holy Spirit. There is an inherent duplicity between what they believe and how they live. They may tell others that Jesus is faithful but when they are in a position where they must walk by faith, they act as if Jesus does not exist. They may tell others that God is more than enough for them until a person of the opposite sex notices them and then they are emotionally unstable. They know that all things work together for their good because they are called according to His purposes, yet when an unexpected crisis occurs they act as if God has forsaken them. These are symptomatic of a lack of integration of the gospel into the emotional standing of a child of God.

We no doubt have heard the statement, "Actions speak louder than words." In many ways, this is very true. The greatest gauge of what we truly believe is how we live our lives on a daily basis. It is easy for us to say, "I surrender all." But it is infinitely harder to lay down something that we have longed for if the Lord were to ask us to do so. It is easy to say, "I love the Lord!" But it is incalculably harder to love the Lord if you are having a Job-like experience. More can be gleaned about what you believe by how you live your life than by what you say about what you believe. I believe this is what Francis of Assisi meant when he said, "Preach the Gospel always and when necessary use words." This does not mean we should never use words when preaching the gospel. Romans 10:17 clearly teaches, "Faith comes by hearing and hearing by the word of God." Rather, Francis is making the point that our lives should already be proclaiming the gospel before we even begin to speak. While evangelicals argue about which translation of the Scriptures is best, we forget that our lives should be the best translation of the Scriptures. We are living epistles that are being read every day in every situation we find ourselves in. Oftentimes, the very people who are unwilling to open a Bible will readily study our lives and with great interest!

I thank God for the Ministry of John Piper. A main emphasis of Dr. Piper's ministry is that a Christian should have abundant joy in God through Christ. I agree wholeheartedly. A Christian's affections and passions should be drenched with the reality of God. As we experience and know God, we should see joy advancing as well. Dr. Piper's passion, his joy, and his satisfaction in enjoying the glory to God are infectious. There is a tangible sense that he is experiencing God in an abundant way and that experience is affecting how he feels and what he desires. This is true of many other great men within Christendom. The risen Christ has profoundly affected their emotional lives. Dr. Piper's message is important for the body of Christ because emotional maturity is important to the emerging worldview. If you go to any local bookstore, you see how large the self help section has become. People, through education and modern psychology, realize how essential having healthy emotions and affections are to their happiness. Also, human emotions reproduce themselves in other people. A person living joyfully will promote joy in the lives of others. The same is true for sadness. It will promote sadness in others.

In the Scriptures, we often find a stout emotional maturity among believers. Only a man whose emotions have been affected profoundly by the gospel can say what James says in Chapter 1 of his epistle; "Count it all joy, my brothers, when you meet trials of various kinds, for you know that the testing of your faith produces steadfastness. And let steadfastness have its full effect, that you may be perfect and complete, lacking in nothing." I do not know how many times I have read this passage and thought that James must have been out of his mind! What kind of a person counts it all joy when trials come upon them? What kind of person enjoys hardship? Simply stated, the answer to that question is the person who knows that God is for him and not against him. The believer knows that God is bearing fruit in his life for God's own glory through present circumstances and in that, a believer greatly rejoices.

Paul says something similar in Romans Chapter 5:

"More than that, we rejoice in our sufferings, knowing that suffering produces endurance, and endurance produces character, and character produces hope, and hope does not put us to shame, because God's love has been poured into our hearts through the Holy Spirit who has been given to us." Paul rejoiced in his sufferings. This is a God-produced emotional maturity indeed! Paul realized and rejoiced that his sufferings would produce hope in his life. A believer can hope because the Holy Spirit pours out the love of God in our hearts experientially. Do you see how knowing God through Jesus Christ radically effects how a believer feels about things?

The Bible is full of instances where the effects of the finished work of Jesus Christ affected the emotional life of a believer. First Thessalonians 5:16 states, "Rejoice always." We are called to be in a continual state of rejoicing. One of the Fruits of the Spirit is joy. We can rejoice always because the Holy Spirit is bearing the fruit of joy in our lives. Jesus said that men would know we are His disciples by the love we have one for another. We often hear in churches that love is a decision, a choice, and not just an emotion. This is true, but love is still emotion. Love is a feeling we have as well as a choice we make.

True Christianity should result in emotional maturity. As we are in the process of growing in Christ, we continually will be conformed into His image. Brothers and sisters let us pursue a gospel-saturated emotional life. Let us pray that God will lead us into emotional maturity that we might be like Christ. At Lazarus's death, Jesus wept for those who wept, as well as for Lazarus himself. Jesus then rejoiced with those who rejoiced. He always did those things that pleased the Father, and that included how He expressed his emotions.

Intelligence and Humility in Spiritual Discussions

Christianity has major intellectual credibility issues in the twenty-first century. In so far as Psalm 111:10 states, "The fear of the Lord is the beginning of wisdom." This state of affairs is a sad indictment on the state of the church. Wisdom begins when a person fears God because God is the ultimate foundational principle. True wisdom cannot be gained unless a person acknowledges God's rightful place as Lord over all. Jesus said that He is the way, the truth, and the life. Jesus is the truth and the foundation for true intellectual credibility. But there are some cogent reasons for our credibility issues today. If we eliminate both the dispersions of those not interested in honest discussions and our own penchant for blame-shifting, those reasons come into specific relief.

First, evangelicals love pithy phrases. It is not that these phrases are false—oftentimes they are quite true. The problem is how we use them. People often have honest questions in regards to faith in Christ. These honest questions are often responded to with trite platitudes or generalized statements. It can be disheartening for a non-believer or person struggling with the faith to ask an honest question and receive a less than thoughtful answer. We have all had experiences in various contexts where we have failed to consider the impact of how we communicate the gospel within our world. Honest questions deserve honest and thoughtful answers.

Second, we often just do not know the answer to a person's questions and instead of acknowledging this, we talk around the question or obfuscate our answers. Rather than considering our answers, or acknowledging something we do not know, we just ramble. There is a reason for the saying that declares, "It is better to be silent and be thought of as a fool then to speak and dispel all doubt." So it is not only that we use pithy phrases, but we often are not mindful at how best to deal with a person's intellectual concerns in a way that makes headway for the gospel. Again, honest questions deserve honest and thoughtful answers.

Third, our credibility issue stems from a lack of true compassion for others. This is not a question of the veracity of what we say, but of the manner in which we say it. A doctor who has a good bedside manner is one who shares the truths of his findings in such a way that validates and empathizes with the fears and concerns of the patient. You know when a doctor has a good bedside manner only after you hear a hard truth from him. It is not that he softens the truth, but that he shares the truth with compassion. Christians lack compassion in sharing hard truths with people. It is not that they say wrong things, but that they share the truth in ways that cause their audience to reject the truth before receiving what is being shared.

God has given each of us a brain with the expectation that we would use it. Jesus said we should be as wise as serpents and as gentle as doves. In the parable of the unjust steward, Jesus taught that we should be shrewd like the steward yet without sin. The apostle Paul, no doubt, was a very intelligent man. He was tactful as well as astute. Even a cursory reading of the Book of Romans shows Paul's keen sense of argument. In fact, Paul's intelligent discourse before King Agrippa and Bernice prompted Festus to proclaim, "Much learning is driving you mad!" (Acts 26:24). The Bible declares that Solomon was the wisest man in history (save Jesus Himself). 1 Kings 3 tells both of Solomon's request for wisdom (that God subsequently grants) as well as a shining example of that wisdom in the case of determining who the remaining child's mother was. The Book of Proverbs, the bulk of which is attributed to Solomon, shows both the depth and vastness of Solomon's wisdom. Solomon's wisdom was so apparent that the Queen of Sheba exclaimed, "It was a true report which I heard in my own land about your words and your wisdom. However I did not believe the words until I came and saw with my own eyes; and indeed the half was not told me. Your wisdom and prosperity exceed the fame of which I heard." (1 Kings 10:6–7). Our mental abilities are given by God and should be used for His glory, honor, and praise.

There is another issue at play. Christendom has allowed there to be a tremendous divide between academic theology and church-based theology. The thoughts and writings of our academic theologians are not making it into the life and theology of the church at large, and the academic theologians are not considering the concerns of the local church. I believe this divide must be closed. When my parents were young, earning a high school diploma was the norm. In my youth, earning a college degree became the norm. Today, earning an advanced degree seems to have become the norm. With each passing decade, Americans are becoming more educated.

With this rise in education, people are more likely to notice flaws in logic and reason and less likely to accept traditional teachings without challenge or debate.

The church has done a poor job of meeting this challenge. We would rather identify whom we should blame for our shortcomings instead of looking at what we can do to be more effective. I believe we need to reevaluate both how we intellectually discuss our faith, as well as the heart in which we express it. Both the intelligence with which we express our faith and the fact that we adequately express the heart and intention of God in our discussions will be a powerful factor in regards to the central tenets of the Integral worldview. Although the Integral worldview is characterized by a smorgasbord spirituality, I am not talking about the more unusual or off-beat New Age beliefs that we have seen historically. There was a time that much of the New Age spirituality was dismissed as too much on the fringe. But now, very well respected and learned people are embracing it within the mainstream. As our culture becomes more and more educated, the church needs to respond with a continued emphasis on ministering Christianity in an intellectually credible way.

It is most encouraging to see that the shift toward a more intellectually credible approach to the gospel of Jesus Christ has already begun. Dr. Timothy J. Keller, the pastor of Redeemer Presbyterian Church in New York City, is at the forefront of this new and necessary development. God is using Dr. Keller profoundly not only to reach New York's up and coming political, business, and social leaders, but also to help equip the body of Christ in communicating Christian truths in a way that, as Dr. Keller would put it is, "both intellectually credible as well as existentially satisfying." [11] Dr. Keller's book, *A Reason for God*, is in my opinion an absolutely essential read. He shares how he learned to communicate these truths through making time for question-and-answer sessions after Redeemer's Sunday services over many years. The sessions were formative in helping Dr. Keller understand and learn how to anticipate the questions of non-believers and seekers about the things of God so that he could address the discussion in his messages. We need more of this in every culture in the body of Christ. We need to anticipate, understand, and address the honest questions of people who do not yet believe in Jesus.

Not only do our sermons and messages need to contain the fundamental, yet dynamic truths of Christianity, but we also must see that the body of Christ is equipped to do this on its own. In the twenty-first century, we need the fulfillment of what is mentioned in James 1:5, "If any of you lacks wisdom, let him ask God, who gives generously to all without reproach, and it will be given him." We need the wisdom of God to be able to both communicate and equip the body of Christ for the task at hand. The church historically has used catechisms to help Christians grow in their faith. In the Greek, *catechism* means, "to sound down (into ears)." It speaks of teaching truths to people. Unfortunately, Christian catechisms are often only theological in nature. This is essential but it is also incomplete.

As the numbers of non-Christians continue to rise, apologetics and evangelism need to be incorporated into our learning. When modernity was at its zenith, classical apologetics were necessary. At that time people disputed the miraculous within the Scriptures and evangelism and apologetics focused on topics such as how we know Christ's tomb was empty and how we can be sure that He was born of a virgin. It was the miraculous claims of the Bible that were under attack by modernity because their reliance on verifiable and empirical data. But among postmodern adherents, these were no longer the battleground issues. As times moved into a postmodern understanding, the church now is just learning what is commonly called presuppositional apologetics. Dr. Keller's book is primarily a manual on postmodern presuppositional apologetics. It approaches the truth of Scripture not from the Christian worldview looking outward, but from the pluralistic worldview looking inward. It begins with what the skeptic believes and then moves to how his belief structure, without Christ, is intellectually untenable. This is why it is called presuppositional apologetics. It begins with the skeptic's presuppositions and its aim is to show how the presuppositions will fail them without Christ. As our culture moves into the Integral Worldview, however, a new and radical apologetic must emerge.

Part of this new apologetic must address the animus of the church toward science. As I have stated, the pendulum always swings. For the better part of the last hundred years the church has taken an adversarial stance toward science, and science toward the church. In some ways this became necessary because of modern science's anti-God posture. But the church's adversarial position is putting Christianity at a distinct disadvantage. It is time for the church to acknowledge the things we can agree on and then intelligently discuss the areas of contention. Again, it is encouraging to see that this is starting to happen in many circles.

We simultaneously are beginning to see many scientists, including non-Christians, who are speaking of how the universe was created intelligently and that it is impossible for the universe to have been created by random occurrences. We are also seeing more Christian scientists writing books and papers with a Christian viewpoint that are being accepted in the secular world. For too long the church has not promoted an intelligent dialogue on many of the differences of thought and opinion with the scientific community. We have been content to sling mud at the scientific community rather than to take the time to engage in robust dialogue. There are men like Lambert Dolphin and Barry Setterfield who have done extensive research, even academically acceptable research, on intelligent design and young earth theory. If you have never heard or read these men, you have a treat awaiting you.

It is important not only that we speak intelligently on these issues, but also that we speak humbly. Hosea says simply that God desires that we walk humbly with Him. If we walk humbly with the Lord then we will also walk humbly with those within our world. It is easy to be proud and boastful against those who hold opposing views, as if they need the gospel more than we do. In reality, however, we need the gospel as much today as we did on the day we first believed. A Christian never leaves a place of complete and utter dependency on God. Because of our awareness of this, our discussions should be tempered by a holy humility. When we proclaim the truth arrogantly, we obscure its truthfulness by our sinfulness. But when we proclaim the truth in humility, the truth will be unhindered. The Lord granted Solomon more wisdom than any person other than Jesus Christ. I believe the Lord wants to grant his people in the twenty-first century in equal measure of wisdom. The gospel is the most intellectually credible worldview in existence because it is the only worldview founded in the absolute truth of God Himself. Intellectual credibility should not be the exception. It should be the rule.

Possessing our Temples with Honor

America is simultaneously the wealthiest and least healthy country in the world. Obesity is on the rise in young and old alike. In some ways, it is the curse of affluence. This affluence has a profound effect on our lives. First, we have access to plenty. We are able to buy things in bulk. Why buy 12 ounces for a dollar when we can get 16 ounces $1.20? Like the Bible teaches, "To whom much is given much will be required." Second, our economy has shifted from a manufacturing model to a service model. Instead of the majority of people doing physical work for eight hours a day, now most people are sitting and using their mental abilities. Combine an abundance of food with a sedentary lifestyle and obesity will rise. This does not even take into account the quality of the food we consume. The problem is that this lack of stewardship over our physical bodies also pervades the church. I have gone to many Christian conferences where gluttony is not only normative but also jokingly encouraged. I have often heard pastors joke about, "just eat the pie and die." Although it makes for a good joke, it makes for lousy witness to the excellencies of Christ. Physical wellness is a necessity. We live this life in a body and our body is the vehicle for our spirits.

In first Corinthians 6:19–20, the Apostle Paul, in speaking of how Christians should avoid sexual immorality states, "Or do you not know that your body is a temple of the Holy Spirit within you, whom you have from God? You are not your own, for you were bought with a price. So glorify God in your body." Paul is teaching that our bodies are the temple in which God's Spirit dwells. He's using the picture of the Jewish Temple to teach a very important truth. The temple, which was designed by David, built by Solomon, destroyed by the Babylonians, and rebuilt by Zerubbabel, and later refitted and expanded by Herod, still stood in Jerusalem as Paul wrote this letter.

When Solomon dedicated the temple in 2 Chronicles 7, you realize that although the building was magnificent, it was only when the Shekinah glory filled the temple that it became a truly spiritual place. What is important is not the building but who dwells within the building. The Spirit who dwells within the temple gives the temple its very meaning. The same is true for our bodies as they have purpose because of the Spirit who dwells within. In every case when there was a revival in Israel because of a godly king, they always sought to tend to the temple that had fallen into disrepair. I am praying for a revival within the body of Christ. As God's Spirit dwells within us, we need to tend to our physical bodies, which have fallen into disrepair.

The question is one of stewardship. As I have noted above, we are created for stewardship. We are created to steward God's creation, our interpersonal relationships (as well as our relationship with the Lord), our blessings, and ourselves. Paul, in his letter to Timothy, told his protégé that bodily exercise was profitable a little but godliness was profitable in all things. Paul is not saying that we should neglect the body in order that we should excel in godliness. It is not an either/or proposition. In many ways this is exactly what the church has done. We have chosen to excel spiritually in godliness, but also have neglected the vehicle through which the Spirit expresses Himself to the world. We are not to be content with simply being physically well. And we are not to be content to be simply godly. It is true that godliness will play itself out in possessing our temples with honor.

As Paul ministered to the church at Corinth, he said, "Whether you eat or drink, or whatever you do, do all the glory of God." In context, he was speaking of offerings and eating things that had been sacrificed to idols. But the truth carries over into our discussion. We should be eating and drinking (or abstaining from the same) solely for the glory of God. We do this because we are not our own. We do this because we were bought at a price. Can anyone honestly say that they are glorifying God in gluttony? Is it possible to promote Christ and at the same time be such tremendously poor stewards of our own bodies? It is possible but only by being duplicitous. We need the gospel of Jesus Christ to integrate into how we possess our bodies. It is so common for us to do a poor job in this area that we pay little attention to it. There is a heightened consciousness of our physical bodies within the Integral Worldview. Many people realize how important good stewardship of their bodies affects the other areas in their lives. This is one of the reasons for the proliferation of the community gyms, as well as establishments devoted to holistic body health.

The concept I am speaking of, Biblical self-stewardship, is not new. Jonathan Edwards, perhaps one of the greatest American minds, spoke extensively about food. In his resolutions, Jonathan Edwards made a point to acknowledge the effects that food has on the spiritual life. His twentieth resolution states, "Resolved, to maintain the strictest temperance, in eating and drinking." He goes on to state in his fortieth resolution, "Resolved, to inquire every night, before the bed, whether I have acted in the best way I possibly could, with respect to the evening and drinking." [12] It was important to Jonathan Edwards that he eats well for the glory of God. We can learn much from Jonathan Edwards in this regard.

There are numerous Biblical examples that continue to challenge us. Third John 2 teaches, "Beloved, I pray that all may go well with you and that you may be in good health, even as it goes well with your soul." The Apostle John here is praying for the physical health of the covenant people. He wants and desires that their bodies are healthy just as their souls are in health because of Christ. Proverbs 3:7–8 goes so far to say that if we fear the Lord and turn away from evil it would be healing to our flesh and refreshment to our bones. As we fear God and experience Him, we will possess our temples with the honor and grace. We often do not equate good physical stewardship with godliness. We see that the Lord wants to promote health in the life of His people and not just spiritual health. True spiritual health will also have immense physical benefits. Do not forget that the Fruits of the Spirit include self-control.

It is essential to understand that body image is a major player in the twenty-first century Western mind. We live in a day and age of eating disorders and many misunderstandings regarding the place of the human body in human experience. Within the church, body image can be equally poor. This ought not to be so. The Scriptures are full of God's prescriptions for what and how we should feed our bodies. The Torah contains many dietary laws. While we know the Bible teaches that all is acceptable if received with thanksgiving, and that the Mosaic laws have been fulfilled in Christ, we need to reevaluate the amount and quality of the food we feed ourselves. Should not followers of Jesus have the healthiest self-image and be God-glorifying in how we possess our vessels? How is it that the body of Christ cares so little for the witness, or better stated, the lack of witness, about how glorious God is by how poorly we possess our own bodies?

I realize that this discussion will no doubt be offensive to some. Why it is offensive might be the bigger problem! If the Fruit of the Spirit is self-control and if fearing the Lord is turning away from evil and healing our flesh and refreshing our bones, then why do we not take greater care of ourselves? If we do not use our freedom as an opportunity for the flesh, we should keep our physical bodies in good working order. When a nonbeliever sees a follower and disciple of Jesus whose temple is in disrepair, it reflects negatively upon the Spirit Who indwells the people of God. You may not like that assessment, but I challenge you to see the truth in it. When someone devalues their mission in life to the point they let themselves become unhealthy, it shows they don't care about the mission. Paul said we hold this treasure in earthen vessels. Our job is to glorify God in our bodies as well as in our minds, emotions and spirits. In some cases it is time for a new diet and workout regimen for the glory of God.

Overflow Interpersonal Relationships

The twentieth century has been marked with a staggering fragmentation in interpersonal relationships. Divorce rates have skyrocketed. Interpersonal relationships have diminished in cultural significance. Conflict resolution is at an all time low. The media and popular culture continually rehash the story that Western culture is coming apart at its interpersonal seams. As we have seen, this truth is the same inside the church as it is outside the church. Divorce rates are almost identical. Very few churches have not had a church split from interpersonal conflict. Christians and non-Christians alike are struggling in their interpersonal relationships. This is happening, in part, because of the self-centeredness of our culture. Some philosophers call the way in which modern people approach their relationships, "the law of reciprocal affection." This means most people are willing to give love only if they receive love in return. "I will give love to you as long as you return it to me. If you withhold your love for me, then I will subsequently withhold it from you." This unspoken precondition leads to misery, not relational fulfillment.

In their book called, *The Lonely American: Drifting Apart in the 21st Century,* Jacqueline Olds and Richard S. Schwartz speak of the continued fragmentation of relationships in American society. Olds and Schwartz are professors of Psychiatry at Harvard Medical School who wrote to confirm the disconnectedness and unhappiness of people in American culture.

> Americans in the 21st century devote more technology to staying connected than any society in history, yet somehow the devices fail us: Studies show that we feel increasingly alone. Our lives are spent in a tug-of-war between conflicting desires—we want to stay connected, and we want to be free. We lurch back and forth, reaching for both. How much of one should we give up in order to have more of the other? How do we know when we've got it right? Two recent studies suggest that our society is in the midst of a dramatic and progressive slide toward disconnection. In the first, using data from the General Social Survey (GSS), Duke University researchers found that between 1985 and 2004 the number of people with whom the average American discussed "important matters" dropped from three to two. Even more stunning, the number of people who said there was *no one* with whom they discussed important matters tripled: In 2004 individuals without a single confidant made up a quarter of those surveyed. Our country is now filled with them. The second study was the 2000 U.S. census. One of the most remarkable facts to emerge from this census is that one of four households consists of one person only. The number of one-person households

has been increasing steadily since 1940, when they accounted for roughly 7 percent of households. Today, there are more people living alone than at any point in U.S. history. Placing the census data and the GSS side by side, the evidence that this country is in the midst of a major social change is overwhelming. The significance of this increased aloneness is amplified by a very different body of research. There is now a clear consensus among medical researchers that social connection has powerful effects on health. Socially connected people live longer, respond better to stress, have more robust immune systems, and do better at fighting a variety of specific illnesses. Health and happiness, the two things we all say matter most, are certifiably linked to social connectedness.

These findings are shocking. Modern medical research supports the notion that we are created for relationship. Despite this, our culture continues to fragment. The first thing God stated was not good was that man was alone. God declared it was not good that man was alone because man was created for relationship; because man was created in the image of God. God is relational in the essence of His being. And being created in the image of God, we, too, are relational at the essence of our being. The Bible shows us both sides of the interpersonal fence. There are shining examples of godly relationships among people. There are also glaring blunders in interpersonal relationships. This is an area that the body of Christ can easily excel if we were to allow the gospel to overflow into our interpersonal lives.

Near the end of the Gospel of John, Jesus speaks of the characteristics of relationships within the body of Christ. The prevailing theme from John 13 through John 17 is that love was meant to be the distinguishing characteristic of the people of God. In John 13:35, Jesus said by this, men will know we are His disciples, by the love that we have one for another. Love was intended by God to distinguish the people of God from others. The difference between a Christian relationship and a non-Christian relationship is the supremacy of the love of Christ in the Christian's life. A Christian's love for another person is not determined by the law of reciprocal affection. A Christian is not to look to another person to fulfill his love needs because his needs have already been fulfilled in Christ. The foundation of a Christian relationship is the love of God that the Christian is receiving through Christ. This love overflows into his other relationships. As a follower of Jesus grows in the satisfying love of God, he is free to love others and enjoy others without the constraints of the need to receive love in return.

Jesus displayed this love vividly. In John 15:12–14, we read, "This is my commandment, that you love one another as I have loved you. Greater love has no one than this, that someone lays down his life for his friends. You are my friends if you do what I command you." The love of Jesus is a giving and self-sacrificing love. This is the lesson of the cross. When a person does not understand the love of God, as displayed perfectly in the cross of Jesus Christ, it is impossible for him to have truly fulfilling interpersonal relationships. This is because he comes into every relationship from a place of deficiency. Every relationship exists to fill a void and thus every relationship is doomed to failure. If a person looks in others for the fulfillment that can only come from God, he cannot succeed in relationships. He is setting everyone up for failure.

But the implications for a believer are staggering! When we understand the cross and the love of God revealed there, we have all of our needs satisfied in the agape of God. We no longer come to interpersonal relationships from deficiency but rather from a place of sufficiency. We must allow the love of God that we are experiencing in Christ through the Holy Spirit to flow through our lives to others. The cross of Jesus Christ radically affects how we relate to people interpersonally. This is why the Apostle Paul went to such great lengths to apply the gospel into differing layers of relationship. Paul discussed marital relationships. He discussed familial relationships. He discussed servant/master relationships. It was important to Paul that the churches of God display the overflowing love of God in their relationships to other people. It is no less important to us today.

Can you imagine the profound effect these types of relationships can have on the church? D.L. Moody was purported to have said that if Christians truly live out the gospel, then there would never be a need for an evangelistic crusade. People would be interested in Christ by the life testimony of His followers. As the body of Christ experiences God, the love of God should overflow by the Holy Spirit, and direct the way Christians relate to one another. The church must find its way back to personal and transformational communities. The Western mindset of individualism has permeated the church in many negative ways. Churches are often cold, cliquish and lacking in authentic relationships. We simultaneously want relationships and resist them. Oftentimes, people would rather come to church than be the church. The body of Christ must cease merely going to church, and return to its roots of being the church. As our culture continues to fragment interpersonally, the church can be as conspicuous as a city set on a hill as we relate to one another in true biblical community. The body of Christ was meant to be a caring, empathetic and transformational community where people are truly connected. The Apostle John said that as we walk in the light as He is in the light, we have fellowship with one another, and truly our fellowship is with Jesus Christ. Because of the unfailing, everlasting love of God that reaches us through the Holy Spirit, we can have true authenticity and intimacy in our interpersonal relationships within the covenant community.

Not only will these relationships overflowing with love affect how churches and our relationships function, but they will also affect how we deal with the disenfranchised and the needy. There is a stereotype that some proponents of the social gospel movement overemphasize tending to the physical at the expense of the spiritual. There are many who will never proclaim the cross of Jesus Christ, yet do abundant social good stealthily in the name of Jesus. Because of this stereotype, many people do not feel comfortable with or have wholly neglected social compassion. But Jesus was the great champion of the needy. He was a voice for the fatherless and the widow. He even turned water into wine so that a bridegroom would not be shamed. The body of Christ must return to social compassion as an avenue to outshine the rest of the world. There are everywhere abundant needs that Christians overflowing with the love of God can address. We all know the parable of the Good Samaritan, but we often neglect the wounded like the Priest and the Levites did. If we heed Jesus's teaching that the greatest commandment is to love God and to love your neighbor as yourself, then we must pick up the mantle of social compassion. Not simply social compassion for compassion sake, rather social compassion as a display to the world of the love of God that is in it to give, and not to get.

Stewardship of the Cosmos

The Green movement is in full swing in America. Sustainability is becoming a way of life. Politicians and pop stars alike are promoting living a green lifestyle. The tragedy of this is that Christians have not been champions of this cause for thousands of years. I have heard many times in many churches, pastors and teachers maligning environmentalism as a New Age conspiracy. Granted, the New Age movement has chosen to worship the creature rather than the Creator, and this is God's judgment on its proponents for refusing to glorify Him as God (see Romans 1). But a Christian should realize the purpose and attributes of nature are the very handiwork of God. It is astounding to me that Christians have not been at the forefront of environmentalism. I will show you biblically how the church has been in gross error on the subject. We will look at both creation and eschatology in order to make this point. Christians should be the best stewards of our God-given environmental resources.

As I have previously written, God created man for stewardship. In Genesis 1:26–30 we read,

Then God said, "Let us make man in our image, after our likeness. And let them have dominion over the fish of the sea and over the birds of the heavens and over the livestock and over all the earth and over every creeping thing that creeps on the earth." So God created man in his own image, in the image of God he created him; male and female he created them. And God blessed them. And God said to them, "Be fruitful and multiply and fill the earth and subdue it and have dominion over the fish of the sea and over the birds of the heavens and over every living thing that moves on the earth." And God said, "Behold, I have given you every plant yielding seed that is on the face of all the earth, and every tree with seed in its fruit. You shall have them for food. And to every beast of the earth and to every bird of the heavens and to everything that creeps on the earth, every-thing that has the breath of life, I have given every green plant for food."

In verse twenty-eight, God gave man the responsibility of stewardship over the created order. He explained to Adam that Adam was to have dominion over every living thing that moves on the earth. God placed man at the top of the food chain to be steward of His creation. God did this and saw that it was good. Unfortunately, man has chosen to exploit the earth rather than be a faithful steward of it. Jesus spoke numerous parables concerning stewardship in the gospels. We often relate these parables to using our gifts and talents, but too often we forget that the very first gift and talent God gave humanity was the stewardship over all He created. We were created for stewardship.

Additionally, Romans 1:20 teaches us that the invis-ible attributes of God are clearly seen, His eternal power and Godhead, in the things that He created. So much so, that all men are without excuse for neglecting to worship Him. Consider the implications of this verse. God's attributes are clearly seen in the cosmos. We have been given stewardship responsibility over God's general revelation, nature. Most Christian scholars acknowledge both God's general revelation in creation and His specific revelation in the Scriptures. We often do well in handling God's specific revelation, but we have a poor track record of handling His general revelation. As we continue to exploit God's creation, we are missing one of our greatest opportunities to share the love of God.

We see this truth in the Psalms as well. Psalm 24:1 states, "The earth is the Lord's and the fullness thereof, the world and those who dwell therein." We are stewards of God's own possession. This includes not only the people who live on the earth but also the earth itself. This is why our stewardship obligation must match the magnitude of that over which we are stewards. If you were to be given responsibility over the Hope Diamond, you most likely would take that very seriously. How much more seriously should you take the stewardship over the rightful possessions of the Almighty? We read in the Psalms that the heavens declare the glory of God. Psalm 150 tells us that the trees of the field clap their hands to God. This is the symbolism used when the Jews waved palm branches at Jesus during His triumphal entry into Jerusalem, signifying creation's joy in the fulfillment of the coming Messiah. Not only is the creation God's own possession entrusted to us, it declares how glorious God is. Christian friend, this is neither an unimportant nor frivolous detail. This is a special responsibility that must be taken seriously.

In Psalm 8, we see the effects of admiring God's created order on the man whose heart is open to the Lord. David says, "You have set your glory above the heaven…

When I look at your heavens, the work of your fingers, the moon and the stars, which you have set in place, what is man that you are mindful of him and the son of man that you care for him?" (Psalms 8:1B, 3–4). David sees the glory of the heavens and thinks about how amazing it is that God is mindful of him. There are many stories told by missionaries of people whose lives testify of the impact God's general revelation had upon them and who freely and joyfully received Christ when Christ was preached to them.

Eschatology also underscores the importance of our need to be godly stewards over God's creation. In Romans 8:19–22, we read, "For the creation waits with eager longing for the revealing of the sons of God. For the creation was subjected to futility, not willingly, but because of him who subjected it, in hope that the creation itself will be set free from its bondage to decay and obtain the freedom of the glory of the children of God. For we know that the whole creation has been groaning together in the pains of childbirth until now." These verses teach that not only will God restore humanity upon the return of Christ, but He will also set the created order free from the decay that resulted from the fall. When Adam fell, the entire created order fell with him. When God created man to have dominion over the created order, as men went, so the created order went. The Revelation of Jesus Christ ends with the ushering in of the new heavens and a new earth. There will be a restoration of the created order in the millennial kingdom. Even if you see the millennial kingdom as a figurative picture, the restoration of creation is still an integrated Biblical concept.

It is unfortunate the Green movement is being led by people who do not acknowledge that the created order is God's own possession, that it declares His attributes, and that it ultimately be restored when Christ returns. The

Integral Worldview places great importance on caring for the environment. Its adherents believe we cannot continue on the path we are on and hope to have a successful future. Christians who have abrogated our stewardship obligations must repent and honor God by our stewardship of the creation that is His alone.

Thinking Points for Pastors and Churches

We have looked at six specific areas that must be reassessed within the body of Christ as we prepare for the Integral Worldview. It now makes sense to consider well the implications this will have for pastors and how we do ministry. The gospel never changes, but the ways in which we can communicate that gospel will continually change as the culture changes. But if Christians walk in true experiential Christian spirituality, have gospel saturated emotional life, intelligence and humility in spiritual discussions, possess their temples with honor, have interpersonal relationships that overflow with the love of Christ, and are faithful stewards of the cosmos, all for the glory of God, changes will follow. This will affect how we minister. Every culture needs a fresh and dynamic display of the finished work of Calvary's cross. The work is finished, the Bible is canonized, and the gospel is unchanging. But how we express these truths to the world is constantly in flux.

The crux of the matter is this: if Jesus were incarnate today what would His ministry look like? How would He relate with your community? And by extension, if the Apostle Paul was making his missionary journeys in your community, where and how would he minister? This is not a simple question; neither does it have a simple answer. Oftentimes, we try to export another person's successful model of ministry in the hopes that we can re-create the unique work God has done in another mission field. Although there is much that we can glean from other ministers and ministries, we can miss what God wants to do in our communities if we do not ask these questions. The answers should be the guide to how we approach ministry.

It is necessary for Christians to remove the *us/them paradigm* from their minds. It seems that we have forgotten from where we have been redeemed. Even though we are born again, we are still sinners saved by grace. We have the same need for a Savior today as we did on the day we were saved. We need the gospel as much now as we did then and that never changes. We are in total and utter need of God's grace at every moment of every day. When we realize that, the us/them paradigm shatters. Nonbelievers can sense spiritual arrogance and pride as we approach them. If we have an us/them mentality, they will see it and frequently will not be receptive to the message we are delivering. The problem applies equally to one on one evangelism as well as teaching from the pulpit.

There have been times immediately before launching a church plant that I was not in church on a Sunday morning. This can be an eye opening experience for a pastor. It is then I realized that vast numbers of people are doing innumerable types of activities instead of attending church. This makes our worship services even more important when we realize the majority of our communities do not believe in Jesus. Ephesians 4:11 teaches that the church was designed for the equipping of the saints for the work of ministry. Church should be a nurturing place for Christians and it should be a dangerous place for non-Christians. I mean dangerous in the sense that their worldviews should be jarred when they hear the teaching of the Scriptures. The church service should also be evangelistic in nature. If we hope to minister and thus fulfill the Great Commission, we need to remember that we are always preaching to a mixed multitude. Because of that, our approach to how we handle the communication of truth will be adjusted. Christians inherently know if their unsaved friends, if they have any, would be able to comprehend the message being shared. We are often content to preach the gospel while forgetting to explain and contextualize it. We often assume that people understand more than they do. Or worse, instead of discussing honest questions about difficult passages, pastors will dismiss as absurd that someone would believe such a thing. Few things will send a seeker running more quickly than having an honest question dismissed or ridiculed by one of the few persons in a position to answer it in a loving, Biblical way.

As contemporary culture continues to progress away from God, we will see more people without the Christian framework to process the gospel. Without a greater effort on the part of Christian ministers to explain that which we take for granted and understand intuitively, we are missing God-given opportunities to evangelize and encourage. I am not advocating diluting the gospel message. We preach the gospel, but often do not realize the words and concepts we are using, many people will not understand. Few postmodern adherents, let alone those holding an Integral worldview, will have the framework to understand concepts like the *Lordship of Jesus Christ*. Few Westerners truly understand it because they have been raised in a democracy where *Lordship* is eschewed. Also, when people hear the word "righteousness" they

often think of self-righteousness, which has negative con-
notations. To remedy this, it only takes a few sentences of
clarification. And in those few sentences, we can build a
bridge for the understanding of the gospel. But we must be
mindful to realize that many people do not have the necessary framework to process the message we are delivering.

Many Christians believe the media loves publicly
scolding ministers who have suffered moral failure.
Although this may be true, the greater problem is that
ministers suffer moral failure at all. It is not as if the media
is framing these people to make it look like they've failed.
Instead, the problem is that they have failed and failed
publicly. We are all sinners saved by grace, but pastors and
churches must lead by example. My pastor, John Henry
Corcoran, has been known to say, "Before you hand me
your tracts, show me your tracks." Christian leaders must
not only occupy the pulpit well, but also walk the moral
high road in both love and grace.

In dealing with culture, churches must either become
separatist or syncretistic. Separatism occurs when the
church completely removes itself from culture and seeks
the solace of the holy huddle. At the other end of the
spectrum, syncretism is where the church begins to incorporate the elements of the world. We see these extremes
today—the church is frequently completely separate or
completely worldly. There is, however, an opportunity
to pioneer a different path. If pastors and churches lead
by example and outshine the unbelieving world in the
ways previously discussed, there is room for God to show
Himself strong. People who have been affected by God
will be effective for God. This was the case in the first
century Church. There were numerous powerful encounters with God through His Holy Spirit and believers' lives
affected the lives of those with whom they had contact.
We must to return to this.

In Conclusion

In Mark 9, Jesus, Peter, James, and John returned to the multitudes after Jesus's transfiguration. They encountered a commotion because Jesus's disciples there were unable to cast a demon out of a young man. Jesus asked that the young man be brought to Him. When the spirit saw Jesus, it immediately convulsed the young man and he fell down with seizure like symptoms. Jesus told the young man's father that all things are possible for one who believes. When the man cried out, "I believe, help my unbelief," Jesus cast the demon out of the young man. Later, Jesus's disciples inquired why they were unable to cast out the demon. Jesus replied that it was of a kind that could not be driven out except by prayer. Some manuscripts indicate that Jesus said both fasting and prayer. In this specific case, in order to do the work of God, something different was required. The way the disciples had done the work was ineffective in this case. Something unique was required here. A new approach was needed because the demon was in too deep. I believe that this is a great picture for doing ministry in an Integral context. The way evangelicals have been doing things previously will not work in the coming decades. The demon is in too deep and new approaches must be uncovered.

I have heard that Dr. Jeff Iorg, the president of Golden Gate Baptist Theological Seminary, located in Mill Valley, California, has said, "The church that will be effective in this generation has yet to be founded. The evangelistic techniques necessary to reach this culture have not been discovered. And the discipleship programs that will nurture a vibrant faith today are not in existence." When I asked Dr. Iorg about this, he told me it is a perpetually true concept. He said he could say the same thing in ten years and it would be just as true. I agree with Dr. Iorg's assessment.

Culture is dynamic. It is in a continual state of change. While the Church obsesses with postmodernism, the postmodern worldview has already come and gone in many respects. It is not easy to stay abreast of cultural changes, but it is an essential mission of the body of Christ. The Integral Worldview, with its integration of multiple truths, is taking root in American culture. The smorgasbord spirituality and syncretism, with its transperspectival and transdisciplinary approach to life, is upon us. We must get ahead of the curve. The truth of the gospel is essential to life.

I want to reiterate that my hope in writing this book is that a robust dialogue will begin within the body of Christ. I have not heard or read any discussion of what follows postmodernism within the church. Unfortunately, what follows is already upon us. Post modernity has come and gone in the Northeast and in the major metropolitan centers of the West Coast. It is firmly entrenched in the central and southern parts of our country. Before long, American culture will be fully integrated. Unless the church of Jesus Christ begins discussing and processing what is already dawning, we will be continually playing catch up. The salvation of souls to the glory of God is too important not to take seriously.

I would like to close in prayer.

> Father, we ask that You would lead us into the truth that is in Your Word, and into a fresh revelation of how to communicate that truth in a changing world. We want to know You experientially. We want to have emotional lives that are saturated with the gospel. We desire Your wisdom and intelligence in discussing spiritual matters. We want our relationships to properly reflect the finished work of the cross. We desire to be good stewards of the things that You created for Your own good pleasure. We also ask that You would teach us how to minister as Christ would minister if He was walking incarnate in the world today. We know that without You we can do nothing. We place ourselves in this discussion in Your most capable hands. Lead us and guide us.

> In Jesus's name, amen.

Endnotes

1 Jon Meacham, "The End of Christian America," Newsweek, http://www.newsweek.com/2009/04/03/the-end-of-christian-america.html (accessed August 14, 2010).

2 Worldviews, Wikipedia, http://en.wikipedia.org/wiki/Worldview (accessed on August 14, 2010).

3 Dr. Timothy Keller, "Preaching to Emerging Cultures," (presented at Ockenga Institute Pastors' Forum, Gordon Conwell Seminary, April 5, 2006.

4 Gary Brent Madison, "The Hermeneutics of Postmodernity and After," Conference on After Postmodernism, University of Chicago, http://www.focusing.org/apm_papers/madison.html (accessed on August 14, 2010).

5 Joe Queenan, *Balsamic Dreams: A Short but Self-Important History of the Baby Boomer Generation* (Picador, June 1, 2002).

6 Dr. Timothy Keller, "The Supremacy of Christ and the Gospel in a Postmodern World," talk delivered at the 2006 National Conference, September 30, 2006, http://www.desiringgod.org/ResourceLibrary/ConferenceMessages/ByConference/36/1832_The_Supremacy_of_Christ_and_the_Gospel_in_a_Postmodern_World/ (accessed on August 14, 2010).

7 "After Postmodernism: A Report," Conference on After Postmodernism, University of Chicago, http://www.focusing.org/apm_papers/conferencereport.html (accessed August 14, 2010).

8   EnlightenNext, December 2008- February 2009, pgs 42–52.

9   Jon Meacham, "The End of Christian America," Newsweek, http://www.newsweek.com/2009/04/03/the-end-of-christian-america.html (accessed August 14, 2010).

10   John Piper, *God is the Gospel*, (Crossway Books, September 8, 2005), http://www.desiringgod.org/Store/Books/ByTopic/All/637_God_Is_the_Gospel/ (accessed August 14, 2010).

11   Dr. Timothy Keller, "Who Is Jesus?" May 1, 1994 message, http://sermons2.redeemer.com/sermons/who-jesus-openforum (accessed August 14, 2010).

12   Jonathan Edwards, "The Resolutions of Jonathan Edwards," http://www.jonathan-edwards.org/Resolutions.html (accessed August 14, 2010).

13 Jacqueline Olds and Richard S. Schwartz, *The Lonely American: Drifting Apart in the 21st Century*,(Beacon Press, February 1, 2010), http://www.utne.com/Spirituality/Reconnect-Technology-Society-Lonely-American.aspx (accessed August 14, 2010).

listen|imagine|view|experience

AUDIO BOOK DOWNLOAD INCLUDED WITH THIS BOOK!

In your hands you hold a complete digital entertainment package. In addition to the paper version, you receive a free download of the audio version of this book. Simply use the code listed below when visiting our website. Once downloaded to your computer, you can listen to the book through your computer's speakers, burn it to an audio CD or save the file to your portable music device (such as Apple's popular iPod) and listen on the go!

How to get your free audio book digital download:

1. Visit www.tatepublishing.com and click on the e|LIVE logo on the home page.
2. Enter the following coupon code: b1ed-b2f8-fdab-a8bf-03f2-e089-6010-1f49
3. Download the audio book from your e|LIVE digital locker and begin enjoying your new digital entertainment package today!